HOW TO THINK AND REALIZE OBJECTIVES UNDER ANY PROPER RULE ENVIRONMENT

A NEW MATH TO UNDERSTAND AND ANALYZE SOCIAL AND ECONOMIC ISSUES

J EDSON LIRA

Copyright © 2022 J Edson Lira.

All rights reserved. No part of this book may be reproduced, stored, or transmitted by any means—whether auditory, graphic, mechanical, or electronic—without written permission of both publisher and author, except in the case of brief excerpts used in critical articles and reviews. Unauthorized reproduction of any part of this work is illegal and is punishable by law.

ISBN: 979-8-88640-175-2 (sc)
ISBN: 979-8-88640-176-9 (hc)
ISBN: 979-8-88640-177-6 (e)

Because of the dynamic nature of the Internet, any web addresses or links contained in this book may have changed since publication and may no longer be valid. The views expressed in this work are solely those of the author and do not necessarily reflect the views of the publisher, and the publisher hereby disclaims any responsibility for them.

One Galleria Blvd., Suite 1900, Metairie, LA 70001
1-888-421-2397

A special thanks to my beloved wife Roseleide Lira and my beloved daughter Nilcea Lira. I surely believe you are part of God's plan for my live; to enable me to endure this long, hard and difficult journey to convey my discovery to as many people as possible, in all social classes around the world.

CONTENTS

1st Edition Presentation vii

2nd Edition Presentation xi

Chapter 1   Waves 1

Chapter 2   Classes 14

Chapter 3   Class Relation 30

Chapter 4   Class Limitations 43

Chapter 5   Imbalance Distribution 52

Chapter 6   Democratic Mode Market 58

Chapter 7   Autocratic Mode Market 76

Chapter 8   Mixed Influenced Mode Market 101

Chapter 9   Controlled Mixed Mode Market 115

Chapter 10 Existential Environment 130

Chapter 11 Existential Dynamics 147

Chapter 12 Democratic Differentiation 162

Chapter 13 Systemic Differentiation 179

Chapter 14 Differential Interactive Waves 192

Chapter 15 Democracy Inefficiency 212

Chapter 16 Democratic Qualitativity 241

Chapter 17 System Analyses 256

Bibliography 267

1ˢᵀ EDITION PRESENTATION

"How to think and realize objectives under any proper rule environment" is possible because of two things; the Game and System Objective Theory and the Lirian Mathematics.

The Lirian Mathematics associates our "thoughts" with "objective values"; and better explains certain economic and social problems. The discovery of the proper rule environment - which is objective and separated from society and nature - has allowed such "advance" in mathematics.

To create this new mathematics the author imported from web programming, some new concepts, which were discovered just in recent years. They are: classes, objects methods, attributes, functions, and variables.

Lirian Mathematics is the first object oriented mathematics that the author knows of. But, there is an important difference, between Lirian Mathematics, and object oriented programming languages. These ones exist and produce objects in a virtual world; while Lirian Mathematics applies to an existential world, subject to "proper rule", "society", "nature", "mental rules", and "decisions".

The Democratic Game and System Objective Theory - that we also call Objective Theory - is a new way to interpret reality.

Instead of creating objective views, opinions, scenarios, descriptions, of reality, based on some one's subjective opinion, the Objective Theory itself is an objective means that allow its user to observe reality as it is; with no interpretation, no second opinion, and no dispute about what is presented.

Conceptually, its major differential is that it is not a "so-and-so think of theory", or "I think that theory", rather it is a systematic, objective, segmented and referenced (by fixed set of principles and concepts), way of watching reality, unreality and our whole life experience. Its concepts constitute themselves, in objects, which have their own existence; in a way that is not dependent upon human opinion.

Another very important differential is that the Objective Theory is a person (system participant) based theory, rather than a social structure based theory like other important theories that are used now in days for reality interpretation. But that does not mean it may substitute them, quite in the contrary Objective Theory is a tool to make such professionals more efficient.

Objective theory does not consider "family", "corporation", or any other social applied sciences structures that we know of. Instead, it considers system participants and proper rule structures that are formed inside the proper rule system; such as rule constructions, schemes, syndromes, and other structural phenomena. This important approach allows its user to "see" things not perceived and not accounted for, with other theories; they, their causes and consequences are perceived only when we use the Objective Theory. We may say the Objective Theory is a theory of "rules, persons and results" either for common or sophisticated people. It applies only to proper rule systems and their relations with other environments; and in this field it is the only appropriate tool for equating and solving rule environment related problems.

This is the 5th text book about this theory, and the first written in English. There are four other text books and two annual democratic indicators books already published in Brazilian Portuguese about this theory and its specific phenomena. But the author has made all possible efforts to present in this book all Objective Theory concepts that are written in prior books, and referred to in this one, so that you may not need to read any one of the prior books unless you want to.

1ST EDITION PRESENTATION

This book is useful for people in any area of activity. Probably it does not demand any knowledge you might not have met in your regular basic education.

With it, you will find a way to organize your thoughts in classes and subclasses. And will find a method to identify classes, class dependences, class rank, and many other classes' characteristics and limitations.

Also you will find a method to relate "thought classes" with "real phenomenon" that apparently are not related, and create "abstract and real class objects".

The autocratic market classification and class analyses presented in this book are very important tools for portfolio managers and all those people who want to maximize returns while doing international applications and investments.

This book will certainly help them spot some new opportunities, and also show some pitfalls that must be avoided.

A study of "consequent" and "interactive" waves, presented in this book constitutes a "must have" tool for people who are worried about social problems. It will help them to avoid "unintended consequences" and "contrary effects", when they present social problem solutions.

Also, class analyses techniques, presented in this book are very important for educators and students in general, because they show how we may organize our "thoughts" in accordance to the way "they naturally organize themselves in real life". This is essential to avoid misses and losses.

Above all, this book is very important for you, who need to vote on elections; be it on stockholder meetings or government system elections.

This text book is a production of the Objective Theory Project, which this author has founded, sponsors, and develops, since November of 2003.

The main objective of this project is to study the Democratic Game and System Objective Theory and produce books that are sold to the general public.

This theory comprehends now three main study areas; Objective Democraciology, that textually describes proper rule phenomena; Lira Method of Objective Evaluation, that uses objective methods to describe the same proper rule phenomenon, in objective forms - such as mathematical relations and indicators, graphs, cartesian charts, computer programming variables, and others; and the Lirian Mathematics which help us to equate and solve democratic- social, economic - problems in a way that is more precise and more adequate.

These study areas are divided into various other parts, each one devoted to a certain group of reality aspects. And they are collectively referred to as Objective Democracy Study Areas, or likewise Objective Theory Study Areas.

2ND EDITION PRESENTATION

Why you must read this book?

First of all; because you need, as much as everyone else, to know the content of this book to apply immediately in your day to day life, in order to act in a way that, more precisely, conforms with "reality" as it presents itself. That means you'll be able to make a better life for yourself, your family, friends, and compatriots; or otherwise submit most of all these people, to imposed losses without being able to act in response.

Second; because many of those who already are making high substantial gains, at this very moment, certainly have noticed – one way or another - that in any substantial relation with other people there are many other aspects involved besides the relation itself.

Third; because your competitors may get acquainted with the content of this book and act in order to make profit or gains at your expense and your compatriots.

What is the content of this book?

The Democratic Game and System Objective Theory (Objective Theory) is an objective segmented and referenced way to observe reality. Instead of creating objective views, opinions, scenarios, descriptions, of reality, based upon some one's subjective opinion, the Objective Theory itself is an objective tool that allows its user to observe reality as it is; with no interpretation, no second opinion, and no dispute about what is presented. Its concepts constitute themselves, objects, which have their own existence; in a way that is not dependent on human opinion.

Objective Democraciology, Lirian Method of Democratic Evaluation, Proper Rule Planning, and Lirian Mathmatics constitute important and unique new areas of study inside this Objective Theory.

This important approach allows its user to see beyond what is daily presented; things that are not perceived and not accounted for, using any other theory. We may say that the Objective Theory is a theory of "rules, persons and results" that apply only to proper rule systems and their relations with other environments; and in this field it is the only appropriate tool for equating and solving proper rule environment related problems.

This book "How to think and realize objectives under any proper rule environment", is the 5th book in this project. It presents to readers, where they are needed, snippets of all prior written books of the author, in order to make this one, easily understandable.

In this book the author presents Lirian Mathematics, which is an entirely new area of knowledge; It uses the concepts of Class, Objects, Functions, Imponderable Factors, Abstract Class Objects, Real Class Objects, Segmentation of Existential Environment; and uses the Perfect Democratic System as a reference. The Lirian Math associates our "thoughts" with "objective values"; and better explains certain economic and social problems. The discovery of the proper rule environment, which is objective and not associated with society or nature, has allowed such "advance" in math. Notice that all figures and numbers, presented are only for illustrative purpose of the ideas proposed on its texts.

Chapters 1 to 4 describes the Lirian Math main concepts; Chapters 5 to 8 presents simple studies of "markets". Notice that "market" is a space where anything, be it real or abstract can be exchanged because Objective Theory recognizes existence as an "infinite dimension environment".

This study displays how one may be losing substantial value in one aspect, but wining big, in some other ways; or vice versa. Indeed, getting poorer and poorer; or richer and richer as time passes!

Chapters 11 to 16 presents Differentiation Concepts (Inequality Formation).

All that in a very simple way to read and understand; designed for, and accessible to, any democratic voter around the world, providing them with this extraordinary tool for bettering their lives. And of course, also for good and bad; public officials, business people, poor, median, as well as rich investors, international community, and others; hopefully to pursue ethical, and sustainable relations with people.

Thank you very much for buying this book and thus bringing life to this project, making it possible for other books to follow up in the Objective Theory area of study.

Have a pleasant reading!

The author

CHAPTER 1

WAVES

01 Introduction

There are certain social and economic phenomena we cannot fully or precisely explain with the existing mathematics. One example of these inexplicable cases, we find in real stock markets.

Today we use two main types of analyses for explaining their price movements – technical analyses and fundamental analyses.

For those who do not know:

Technical Analyses consists in accompanying market prices to detect some eventual imbalances among demand and offer. If eventually there is lower demand; prices dip. And may rebound when there is higher demand. We can have these analyses done for short, medium and long periods; for the whole market, for parts of it and for isolated papers. Thou in "bear" periods we have low demand and in "bull" periods we have high demand.

Fundamental Analyses consists in studying all data coming from the market, including balance sheets, results and other information, along with any news that may impact the market, All this to detect imbalances among prices and return. For instance, we may check the ratio price/return – present or expected; when there is excess return, prices tend to go up; but if they plunge, then prices tend to follow. Also we can make these analyses for short, medium and long periods; for the whole market, for parts of it, and for isolated stocks. Lower returns mean lower prices, and higher returns mean higher prices.

Notice that in these two types of analysis we consider market movements as a result of its participant's natural interaction. Or in other words, we believe that participants themselves and all together, determine demand and price conditions for the market.

But if you watch carefully for some time any real market, mainly when it exists in a deficient or inefficient environment, you'll soon perceive, that these two types of analyses considered isolated or together, do not fully explain its price behavior.

Many times, in most of real stock markets, price movements end up some times, being a big surprise for technical or fundamental analysts. Prices go up; when they thought they should go down, and vice versa. Sometimes, stark price fluctuations simply have no explanations in their analyses.

All this means that in spite of the two method of analyses currently being used a real stock market end up showing up a great deal of uncertain movements. That is, they don't completely conform to these analyses.

We find other example of nom conformation to actual analyses in real government markets. For instance, in many countries; government officials try restlessly to reduce poverty, but only to watch it increase constantly. They use all kinds of research, to guide their decisions. But still they don't get the results they want, or worse they get contrary results.

02 Lirian Mathematics

Lirian Mathematics uses a mathematical view of proper rule system phenomena; and allows us to equate them, using imponderable factors, and find solutions that are more precise and adequate. The objective of this book is to show you how to get this done.

Its specific scope is the same defined in the Democratic Game and System Objective Theory, which we shall refer to in this book simply as Objective Theory.

The Objective Theory consists in an objective, segmented, and referenced way of watching reality as it is. So, its methods are objective, but reality is always considered as we find it. There is no rhetoric, no interpretation, description, no vision or whatever.

Its methods include the "proper rule system" concept, a fixed set of principles called democratic characteristics, and a series of abstract segmentation of reality in environments, dimensions, classes. All this we shall discuss thoroughly in this book.

We call "proper rule system" to a set of three basic parts that are always present whenever we create or we find a set of rules to be enforced by someone and obeyed by others. The following figure 01, illustrate these parts:

Proper Rule System		
Set of Rules	Actuating Environment	Consequent Environment
Rule Space	Rule Environment	

A proper rule system is formed by a set of rules - that contains the official rules; an actuating environment formed by all actuating agents;

and a consequent environment formed by all consequent agents – who fulfill system orders.

Systems that exist to govern all people in a region are called government proper rule systems, and their basic parts assume different names: Set of Rules is called Democratic Thinking, or Law; Actuating Environment is called Government; Consequent Environment is called Democracy. Government means all government officials referred together. Democracy means all consequent agents referred together. Notice that, Objective Democracy is another concept that we shall refer further in this book.

In democracy we find democracy markets – controlled by consequent agents; and government markets – controlled by government agents.

What differentiates the proper rule system from society is its objective nature. Just because of this, any Objective Theory phenomena may be presented in any objective form; such as mathematics, algebra, graphic, analyses, account, and computer language. It may also be presented in a simple representation of any of those ones. Notice that every one of the infinite aspects that constitute existence environment is by nature class independent from all the others; aspects are separate ways of thinking about things. And all things that exist have infinite values in every one of these infinite aspects of existence.

We call **Objective Democracy Sciences** to all study areas based upon the objective theory. Its main areas are as follows; Objective Democraciology – that studies proper rule systems phenomena in a descriptive way; Lira Method of Objective Evaluation – that compares real proper rule systems phenomena with ones in a perfect or more efficient system. Proper Rule Planning – that studies the various classes of system organizations. And the new area presented in this book; The Lirian Mathematics.

In this book the author shows readers some proper rule phenomena that are present in democratic, government, tax and service markets, and the whole proper rule system. They all have an interesting relation with each other through the common system where they exist.

03 Imbalanced Equations

Follow these thoughts:

A government determines that poor people shall pay less and rich people shall pay more for the same public service they receive.

Consider a public service that costs 1.000 dollars to a rich person that uses it. And that this same service costs only 50 dollars to a poor person that also uses it, in the same place.

These values can be inserted in a greater amount of tribute, paid by the rich, and in a minor amount of tribute paid by the poor.

Consider that this service costs to the government 100 dollars. Then, if we objectively express these facts in mathematic expressions, we will have the following, in dollars:

$$\text{Service} = 100$$
$$\text{Service} = 50$$
$$\text{Service} = 1.000$$

That is:

$$\text{Service} = 100 = \text{Service} = 50 = \text{Service} = 1.000$$

Eliminating the "Service" in excess, we have as follows:

"Service = 100 = 50 = 1.000": (not logical!)

For which there is no logical explanation.

But in our day to day life nobody disputes that the fact described by these expressions occurs. So, these are real expressions!

There are many government proper role democratic systems where services are charged in different values as a function of different social-democratic classes of their participants.

04 Objective treatment of this matter

Until now people has chosen to consider in these equations some specific value of discount or surcharge that objectively equates them.

And they deal with these cases as a matter of simple data manipulation. These data are pre-established, or pre-determined by some mathematic role made by them. For instance those expressions of our example could become like this:

$$\text{Service} = 100 = (50 + 50) = (1.000 - 900)$$

Or we may write it in another way:

$$\text{Service} = (100) = (100-50) = (100 + 900)$$

Expressing it in this way, they may establish a table, or a formula, or some objective expressions that suggest the variation of the objective factors added or subtracted to the cost, as a function of alterations in other variables included in such set.

In doing so, we are simply trying to find an objective solution for a matter that in reality involves subjective control of authorities.

It's as if we are trying to write an expression to define what a person is going to do tomorrow. But each person is free to do whatever he or she can and wishes to do!

To try to minimize their constant mistakes, some people use various scenarios in their calculations. Each one based upon different context of variables, and presenting different solutions for the same matter.

Thousands of people doing calculations; means thousands of scenarios, calculus, and different values for the same matter. And many times, real thing turns out to be very different from all that was calculated!

05 Actuating Subjective Equations

That happens because the control of that matter is not in the hands of those who are doing the calculation, but it is in the hands of the authorities. That can decide by infinitely different ways. And any decision causes infinite repercussions in the democratic environment.

So, the matter presented to you in this example, cannot be properly understood under objective mathematic that we know of today. Exactly because it involves not only objective aspects, but also subjective aspects, that are mathematically imponderable. In this case it involves "a decision from authorities in control of the system, to charge different prices, for the same service.

This is precisely the realm of subjective class equations, or simply class equations.

We call an equation, subjective when at least one of its members contains an imponderable subjective factor, in the objective mathematical environment.

So, let's equate the same problem using subjective equations:

Consider:

$Service$ = real service cost
$Service_1$ = minor price
$Service_2$ = major price

The values are:

$Service$ = 100 dollars

$Service_1 = 50$ dollars
$Service_2 = 1{,}000$ dollars

That means the authority that controls the service decided to diminish 50 dollars in the price for those that are poorer ($Service_1$), and increase 900 dollars for those that are richer ($Service_2$).

When we add the values introduced by the decisions, the numbers go like this:

$Service_1 = 100 - 50 . Decision_1$
$Service_2 = 100 + 900 . Decision_2$

In these two subjective class equations, Decisions 1 and 2 are imponderable factors, because they do not enter in the calculations. They just introduce in the equations the objective values (-50) and (+900).

When Imponderable Factors are active they assume value 1 and when they are not active they assume value 0 (active=1; inactive = 0). In this case they are active and really introducing values in the equations.

We call Objective Factors to the values that are introduced in equations by imponderable factors.

Thus in all subjective equations we have imponderable factors and objective factors.

Objective values depend on the will of those who introduce them, and not on the will or expertise of anyone who makes the calculation.

That means a part of the solution of this kind of problem is the analyses of the imponderable and objective factors involved in the equations.

Now we can relate all values with each other using the subjective imponderable factors and their respective objective factors, as follows:

$$\text{Service} = 100 = 100 - 50. \text{Decisão}_1 = 100 + 900. \text{Decisão}_2$$

If imponderable factors are inactive ($\text{Decison}_1 = \text{Decision}_2 = 0$) than we have:

$$\text{Service} = 100 = 100 = 100$$

This makes complete sense, in the democratic environment.

06 Trans-Environmental Equilibrium

We call disequilibrium to each imponderable factor and respective objective value. We say that these equations – originally balanced – assume an imbalanced form due to disequilibrium of subjective nature introduced by interaction, with other environment. In this case, the environment that receives the action from authorities is the consequent environment, or democracy. And the environment, from where the imponderable factors are coming, is the Actuating Environment, or Government. The following figure 02 illustrates this imbalanced interaction:

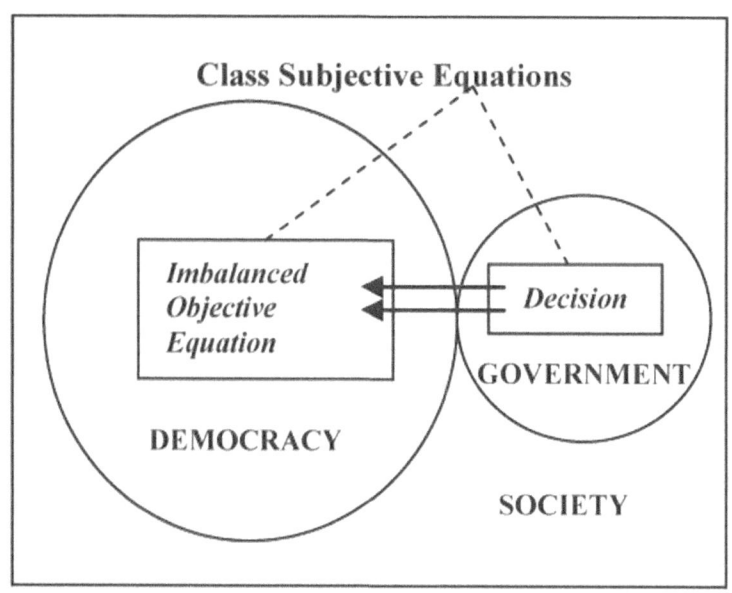

We observe in this representation that one member of the class equation is located in Democracy and the other is in Government. This is a Subjective Class Equation because one person, who possesses capacity, imposes disequilibrium against the Consequent Environment. But this matter is not finished yet. Please follow this thought in the next section.

07 Consequent Subjective Equations

When we consider disequilibrium, then the problem of objective values seams solved.

But when we broke the equilibrium in the objective equation, in reality, we created an "objective factor" that imposes a "new" disturbance in the social environment. And this disturbance may affect all infinite aspects of Society Environment.

To compensate this disequilibrium, "new" social imponderable factors are activated in the Social Environment, and affect back the Consequent Environment.

They produce pressure on it to move value in a contrary sense of the actuating action.

These social factors end up creating in the Consequent Environment a "half wave" of imbalanced equations tending to neutralize the imbalanced effect of the actuating subjective equation.

For instance, in this case, it goes as follows:

Subjective Actuating Equation

$$A + A_2 = D. \text{Decision}_{government}$$

Equation that is formed as a consequence: $B - B_2 = R. \text{Reaction}_{social}$

Where; B represents other service; and R. Reaction $_{social}$ represents a disequilibrium added by social imposition.

And if we consider that:

$$D. \text{Decision}_{(government)} = R. \text{Reaction}_{social}$$

Then we have that: $(A + A_2) - (B - B_2) = 0$

Thus, these equations referring to value of services A and B, that seemed to be simple, isolated, and imbalanced equations in the democratic environment; when we take into consideration their relationship in the government and social environments, we perceive that they balance each other, forming a "complete wave" with zero resulting value.

In other words, these equations are imbalanced, but the complete wave they form, presents itself balanced in the consequent environment, with zero net result.

These equations formed by reaction to a subjective actuating equation are called consequent subjective equations. They may involve many different services in the same consequent environment.

So a wave is formed by imbalanced opposing equations that relate to each other in other environment. In this case we have a balanced wave, but we also may have a wave conveying an imbalance in any aspect. The following figure 03 explains this thought:

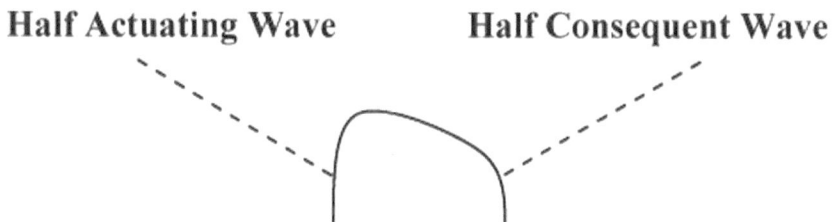

Half Actuating Wave   **Half Consequent Wave**

We call this wave by the name of **actuating wave**. But this is not the end for this matter; please see the next section.

08 Interactive waves

But the formation of this new imbalanced equation brings with it new "objective factors" that disturb again the Social Environment.

Even thou it balances the actuating imbalanced equation making disappear any imbalance in the Democratic Environment, these new objective factors created inside it, shall be disturbing again the Social Environment.

For instance, let us suppose that a government imposes a tax increase P against an industry Z. And that in return this industry reduces the salary of its workers by (-P). This means that the economic equilibrium in its wave (industry) was reestablished. So, there is no disequilibrium when we consider only those two subjective equations.

But the reduction of salaries became itself an objective factor to disturb the Social Environment. And enacts in it, new social factors that by their turn, cause additional disequilibrium in the Democratic Environment, including the very industry Z.

For instance, its workers, who got a K reduction in their pay check, may diminish their production by (-D).

Or they can demand the presence of a new employee at the cost of (-T), just to force then to produce the same amount as they did before, or maybe; a combination of both.

Continuing our example, productivity reduction (higher production cost), becomes a new objective factor to disturb the Social Environment, creating in it new social factor which creates back new imbalanced equations in the Democratic Environment. Also, a lesser amount of salary in the wallet of workers becomes new objective factor of disturbance of the social environment, which also creates back in the democratic environment new imbalanced equations.

These new imbalanced objective equations by their turn, each one brings with it self new objective factors that create new social factors that in turn creates back new imbalanced equations in the Democratic environment. And the cycle of disturbance and reaction goes on, reaching an uncertain number or even all infinite aspects of the Democratic Environment.

We call all these new equations formed after the actuating wave by the name of Interactive equations. They constitute **interactive waves**. The following figure 04 explains these thoughts.

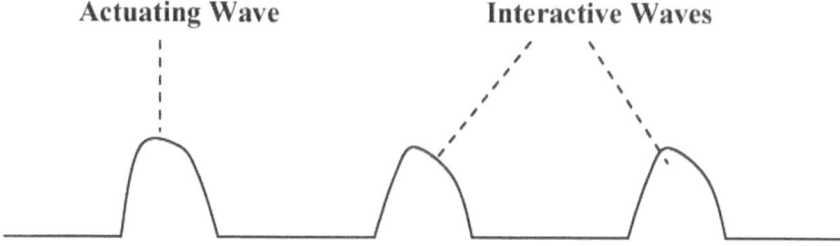

This figure shows that any imbalance introduced in the democratic environment forms actuating and interactive waves that propagate its effects throughout all its infinite aspects. That constitutes the **imbalance propagation principle.**

CHAPTER 2

CLASSES

01 Class

We call **class** an abstract idea about something. For instance: fundamental teaching; 4ª grade; fight against violence; huger; wealth; building; house; social equalization; social justice; faithfulness, etc.

These are some characteristics of classes:

1. A class has no material existence because it is only an idea.

2. Classes do exist in the Mental Environment, where they have infinite coordinates which define aspirations, intensions and desires.

3. Classes are created or extinguished without real action power conversion and without resource mobilization.

4. Classes have their own characteristic or class variables that separate themselves from all other thoughts.

5. All classes can be instantiated in the conceptual dimension of a democratic system, and some classes can be instantiated in reality.

6. This possibility of instantiation conveys to classes the faculty of being able to relate one to other, different identities or objects.

For instance; "human being" relate to (Mary; Paul); "house" relate to (green house; blue house).

7. This possibility of instantiation also confers to classes the faculty of being used as abstract references for real objects.

8. The proper characteristics of a class are intrinsic to itself, but we can identify and describe them in so many aspects as we wish. For instance; a 4° grade in natural aspect must have; pupil, teacher, didactic material; in the regulation aspect must contain a government licensed didactic program for the curse. And in social aspect it needs to comply with a scientific study.

9. Trough instantiations of classes we may create real situations with infinite real coordinates.

10. Classes constitute themselves as options at our disposal to be realized or not.

Classes exist in our mind, but they have their proper characteristics that separate each one from all other ideas. For instance; when we speak about a "building", we produce an abstract form of this idea in our mind.

When we speak of "happiness", immediately we mentally relate some feelings with this concept. This is exactly the functions of classes, that is to separate things in our mind. Naturally, mental ideas formed by different people are also different. But the important thing for classes is to separate things in our mind, and not their identification which is a function of class objects.

Let us analyze certain aspects of these characteristics.

We say that a class relates to another when causes its existence or has its existence caused by that class.

When a class causes the existence of other classes, we say it is an option.

When a class exists because of the existence of other class, we say it is a dependence or subclass of that class.

When a class, is instantiated together with another class, and is not its dependence then we call it interactive class.

02 Subclasses

Subclasses give subjective or objective configuration to classes. In other words, they form the parts that constitute classes.

For instance:

(Option) **Class:**

Apartment Building

(Dependences) **Subclasses:**

Architectural subclasses
View
Facade
Side View
Ceiling
Etc.

Environment subclasses
Apartment
Living Room
Dormitory
Kitchen
Etc.

Structural subclasses

Beam
Pillar
Etc.

Any subclass may be referred to as a class when we are referring to it as an option, independently of other class. Example: Class (dormitory); which has as its subclasses, all ideas of things that go into a dormitory - such as wardrobe and others.

03 Interactive Classes

The interactive classes give functionalities to classes, without belonging to them.

For instance:

(Option) **Class:**

Apartment Building

Interactive Subclasses:
Engineering services
Welders
Masons
Electricians
Etc.

Selling Services
Real sellers
Economists
Etc.

Operational Services
Porters
Cleaners
Watch men
Etc.

04 Class Instance

Instantiate means define or construct an identity relative to a class. This includes a precise definition – with coordinates, quantities, and values – of a particular class, and its subclasses. An Instance is an abstract or real identity, related to a class. It is formed as a result of a class instantiation process.

We may call Subjective Classes to subclasses belonging to a class, which were chosen for instantiation, among all subclasses also belonging to the same class.

For instance:

(Option) **Class:**

Apartment Building

(Dependences) **Subclasses:**

Apartment

(Dependences) **Apartment Subclasses:**

Living room
Balcony
Dormitory1
Dormitory2
WC1
WC2

In this example the instantiator subjectively chose living room balcony etc to instantiate together with the subclass apartment.

To instantiate a class, we need to instantiate one, some, or all of its subclasses. We cannot instantiate a class without subclasses, and we cannot destroy a class which is instantiated without destroying its subclasses.

05 Abstract Instance
Abstract Class Object
Class Project

After definition of subjective classes, the instantiator goes on to define the exact dimensions and other specifications of the object he wishes to create.

The abstract instantiation consists on impression in any auxiliary means - be it an analytical form, or a digital form, or a design, or a combination of various means – of the greater amount of data that is possible, referring to the object he wishes to create.

We call Abstract Class Object or Class Project to the result of an abstract instantiation.

A class project has the following characteristics among others;

1. It does not have real existence. It is constituted of an abstract idea that is (partially) expressed in an auxiliary means. It exists in people's minds.

2. Constitutes itself of a class with its subclasses, coordinates, quantities, values, and specifications precisely defined. For instance: project of a new port; project of a new social class; project of a new regulation; etc.

3. By principle, they have an identity correspondence to, real class objects which were realized after them or that they represent in an abstract dimension. That means a project must describe its correspondent real class object in all characteristics.

4. But any real phenomenon has an infinite number of coordinates, and it is not possible to express them all in any project. Because of this, there is a syndrome called "project syndrome" which states; "in any class project there are an infinite number of

coordinates that are absent". And all these absent coordinates need to be instantiated together with the others in the project to form a real class object. That means they must be defined in the process of real instantiation.

By other side, we may create separate class objects to separately instantiate some subclasses, supplying precise information abut the class they relate to. For instance: illumination project; gain project; legal demands project; etc.

06 Real Instance
Real Class Object
Realization of Class
Real Situation

We call real class object or class realization, or yet real situation, to the result of an instantiation of a class project.

Many conditions need to be met, before we are able to instantiate a class in reality.

Among them the following:

Conditions for realization of a real class object:

1. **An abstract Class Object** – normally we cannot realize an idea, if we do not know precisely, its class and subclasses. Mainly that is true, when we realize things for other people in a professional fashion. From there comes the need of pre-existence of an "abstract class object" referring to whatever object we intend to realize.

2. **Altering Reality** – when we realize a class object, we alter the environment related to it. To Alter something, means to imbalance and then balance again in a different way. We alter an environment to construe or destroy something. To construe

means to alter an existing situation to a new one with more subclasses. For instance, we construe when we transform a naked piece of real estate (with few classes), into an apartment building (full of classes and subclasses). To destroy means to alter an existing situation into another with fewer classes. For instance, destruction occurs when we destroy a house.

3. **Presence of a Method** – we need to know the method used for realization of a class object and its subclasses. Or else we need to know someone who knows that. The action power conversion principle makes it possible to convert one form of action power into another. Thus we can convert economic power into technical action to realize a class. These technical actions in turn may convert to reality a "class project" we want to.

4. **Presence of Power** – we need power in the, rules, social, natural, mental, and sovereignty environment to be able to realize a "class project". For instance, in the rule environment we need clearance from government. In the society environment we need capital, and neighborhood acceptance. In nature we need space, time and other natural conditions.

5. **A set of class equations** – when we want to realize an "abstract class object" or modify a "real class object" we need to solve a system of class equations; subjective equations, impersonal equations and some objective equations. For example: "Violence Extinction" = 500 dollars

This is an actuating class equation where someone intends to transform the abstract class object "violence extinction" into a "real class object", by dispending in the process that amount of dollars. This realization will only be possible if the "real instantiation cost" for this "abstract class object" is less than that value.

07 Relating an idea with Reality

We may transform ideas in reality. The first step to do this is to have an idea, than to transform it in a project and finally to transform this project in a real object.

$$\text{Idea} \rightarrow \text{Project} \rightarrow \text{Real Object}$$

This constitutes the way to class realization. We can observe that the relationship of project to real object is one that occurs by identities. That is, aspects represented in the abstract class object and its correspondents in the real object must have identical values.

But to relate an idea with an abstract object we find a problem. Idea is an abstraction that by its nature is imponderable, while abstract class object demands the expression of quantities, and values in every aspect in the exact dimension they will appear in the real object. To solve this kind of problem we use class equations.

08 Class Equations

Class equation is one, where there is at least one imponderable idea as part of any of its members. They serve to relate idea with objective value. A class equation may be subjective or impersonal.

Subjective class equations are those ones where a person with capability for such, actuating as an imponderable factor, determines the introduction of some objective factors in an objective equation.

Impersonal class equations are those ones where an impersonal agent (from rule, social, nature, mind or sovereign environment), actuating as an imponderable factor, causes the introduction of objective factors in an objective equation. For example, hurricanes, plagues, etc.

Objective Theory, by objectively defining the rule environment, and segmenting reality in separate environments and dimensions, allows us to use class equations for solutions of democratic problems, social – democratic problems, and for solutions of natural – social – democratic problems.

A democratic matter refers only to rules; a social – democratic matter refers to the relation among rules and social environments; and a natural – social – democratic matter refers to problems involving natural, social and rule environments.

The day to day dimension constitutes a real instance of an "abstract class object" represented by the "consequent environment added with consequent dimension". Which ones in their turn, relate themselves with the concept of "objective democracy".

09 Characteristics of Class Equations

1. They exist to help us to organize our thoughts and realize ideas that may be realized.

2. They always present then selves in huge quantities in all social problems. Where there is one class equation, there are many of them.

3. They form waves of different classes.

4. Each wave balances some ideas and causes the appearance of other waves.

10 Solution of a Class Problem

The solution of a class problem involves:

1- Class analyses
2- Class equations
3- Objective class Equations
4- Solution of all objective equations

So, considering the cited class equation we have that:

"Extinction of violence" = 500,000 dollars

First, we need to elaborate a class analyses to determine all subclasses, and interactive classes involved in this matter. After that we need to construe an "abstract class object" that represents all alterations we want to realize. For this, we shall be taking into consideration all imbalanced equations that precisely express all alterations, consequences and interactions that need to occur.

The object cited in this example may not be realized if its instantiation cost is greater than that cited value. Any obstacle (sovereign, mental, natural, and social or rule environment) may hinder our intention to instantiate in reality an "abstract class object".

Also, when we try to instantiate in reality an "abstract class object", we may end up instantiating another object, inclusive one, that we did not want to instantiate. That may occur due to various factors, including errors in class analyses, or not consideration of some imbalanced consequent or interactive equations, or simple calculus errors.

11 Waves

As we said before, a wave is a set of seemingly imbalanced and disconnected equations, but that balance themselves one over the other through an imponderable factor belonging to another environment. That means whenever we speak about a wave, we are referring ourselves to a multi environment structure.

The waves are abstract rule system phenomenon which have correspondent real phenomenon in the social, or natural environment. When they are recognized in reality, they may have social names; for instance, a corporation, a family, a real state, etc. And in some cases, they may have real correspondent in the same rule system too; for instance, "the system administration".

Therefore, a wave is an "abstract class object" of a "real class object" that really occurs in reality. So being, it has infinite aspects and coordinates that normally are not objectively expressed. It is just like the "project of an apartment"- it never contains all coordinates no matter how much detailed it is. By the other side, it may be represented even by a single number, yet it is there with all its infinite aspects and coordinates. And it relates to a real event in day to day life that exists already or is to be built someday.

The waves, present themselves in different forms. That allows us to classify them according to their **formation, objective** and **structure** as follows:

12   Wave according to its formation

A wave may be an actuating or interactive wave according to its formation.

Actuating wave - is formed by actions and reactions of actuating and consequent agents.

Interactive waves - are formed naturally in the democratic environment as a consequence of the existence of the **actuating wave**.

Example, the idea of a "house construction" is an **actuating wave**, but the idea of "people that come to effectively build its various parts" constitute **interactive waves**.

13   Wave according to its instantiation

A wave may be classic or object wave according to its instantiation.

A classic wave is expressed only by the classes involved in it.

An object wave is expressed by objects involved in it.

But notice that waves are only partially expressed. An object wave may be expressed as its correspondent classic wave, and both of them may be expressed with more components to reflect a wider range of aspects involved.

14 Wave according to its objective

A wave may be an **Imbalance** or **Class Wave** according to its objective.

Imbalance waves are naturally formed to balance disturbances that occur in one environment with an opposite disturbance in other environment.

For instance, a government imposes a tax hike over a family and this family reduces social spending – such as "desist of painting their house".

They are natural instruments for conveying imbalance effects through different environments.

Class Waves constitute themselves by a group of different class equations, which are integrated in a system with a certain objective.

They occur as a function of an existing "need" or "opportunity" or an "idea", that is common to their participants.

For instance, a corporation is a class wave that is basically formed in the social environment but balance itself with its part inside the democratic system.

Democratic systems state the norms for these companies to officially exist, and their waves balance themselves.

Democratic values – those that are presented because of government rules – coming from a corporation, represent its "state of democratic balance". Which one, may be complemented by another "state of social balance" in this same wave.

In real environment an informal business is a wave that exists and balances itself solely in the very social environment. Notice that real environment is comprised of rule, society and nature environment.

But if we consider this same informal business in existential environment (reality plus unreality) than it balances itself on trust to one another of their participants; that means mental environment. Notice that unreality is comprised of mental and sovereign environments.

It is an abstract balance that may change without resource mobilization at any time.

Notice that:

1. "Class wave" is an abstract conception about abstract or real objects, which exists only in the mental environment.

    Nobody is able to watch one of these in day to day life. Their objects may be seen on the ground, but not the mental relation among them.

    For instance; we may see the installations, the employees, the owners, by laws, the other material from one particular company, but we are unable to see the mental relations that binds them all together – and integrates its class wave. All that may be seen only through representation.

2. A corporation wave may be partially represented by its Statements, such as the ones we find in our day to day life. For instance:

    Result Statement Company X, period Z;

    Gross profit
    Tax
    Merchandise
    Work

Net Profit
Imbalance

3. These values are "abstract class objects" out of subclasses that form a **Class** (Result Statement Company X period, Z), as it is expressed.

4. But besides these expressed "abstract class objects", this wave contains many others that simply are not expressed, nor are mentioned their respective classes.

5. We may express a class wave with as many aspects as we desire.

15 Wave According to its Structure

A wave has a multi environment structure. Thus, besides reaching out to the rule system's agents, it also encompasses all that exists. That is, rule agent's attributes, social and natural agents and their attributes.

For this reason, we may classify waves according to their structures as attribute waves, agent waves, both agents and attribute waves, and waves of waves.

For instance, if we consider relations among teacher and pupils, than we have an **agent wave**. If we consider an apartment, or a car, they constitute **attribute wave**. If we consider a public transportation, then we speak of an **agents and attributes wave.** And finally if we consider a football match, than we are speaking of a **wave of wave**; among them teams, audience, stadium etc…

Notice that:

1. Attributes belong to someone. That is, attribute classes are normally subclasses from some agent class.

2. That means many waves that are expressed solely by attribute class objects, in reality do not constitute an attribute wave, because they have hidden in themselves the agent classes to whom these attributes belong.

3. For instance, in the wave "Result Statement Company X period Z" is not expressed the agents who control each and every one of these attributes. But they do exist and must be considered in any calculations about this wave.

4. But the "sky above us", a "bee colony", a "geographic event", all these are attribute waves whereas they have no "existing owner".

CHAPTER 3

CLASS RELATION

In this chapter we shall discuss a little more about classes and their dependences.

01 Class Analysis

Class analysis is the study of characteristics present in a class that are useful to us; including its relations to other classes, and its dependences. Let us do some class analysis as we move on.

02 Analysis Class (Right to Vote)

The right to vote is a class created and defined by rule. One of its characteristics is its individuality; that is, the right to vote is personal. But in order for your vote to be counted, there has to be an election. That means the content of a vote is dependent from the existence of an election. With relation to election we have that:

Class (Election)
Subclass (Right to Vote) – is dependent of class (Election)

But Class (Election) has other dependent classes that include rights to vote relative to all other electors. Let us consider that there was an election and that you and your neighbor cast your vote on the ballot box. If we do not take Class (Election) into consideration, then relation between your vote and your neighbor's vote goes like this:

Class (**Right to Vote** (Your Vote)) – is independent
Class (**Right to Vote** (Your neighbor' Vote)) – is independent

That means without class (Election), your right to vote is independent from your neighbor's vote. Precisely from this situation comes the erroneous notion that your vote is free and independent. But when we take Class (Election) into consideration, things change, and relations are these:

Class (Election)
Subclass (**Right to Vote** (Your Vote)) – is dependent
Subclass (**Right to Vote** (Your neighbor' Vote)) – is dependent

So, the act of going to the poll may be free and independent but the value of your vote in reality relates to your neighbor' vote through the **Class (Election)**. And this dependence, is present on election' result. The following figure 05 illustrates this thought:

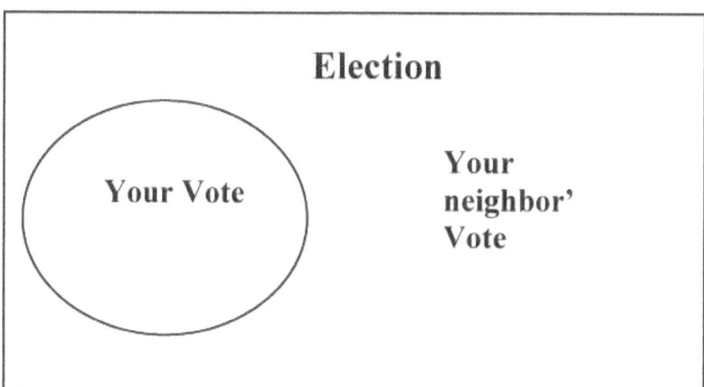

03 Analysis Class (Election)

Now let us discuss something about class (Election). Once an election is established, it evolves by its own rules. If these rules uphold the democratic principles - sovereignty with the elector, freedom of information, rule of law, submission of authorities, and responsibility - then we can say the election is free and democratic.

But in reality, elections occur in places where information is censored, electors are threatened, authorities rig the results, electors exchange their votes for money, and many other deficiencies. And in spite of all this, there are many people, who call them free and democratic. In all these cases, these people are only using concepts that they invented, but that have no relation to the democratic principles.

But why would any people hinder the electoral process? They would do that precisely to take advantage of the dependency of Class (Right of Vote).

Notice the following example; there are 500 people registered to vote in an election. And they must elect the 5 most voted candidates.

Let's suppose that there are 20 eligible candidates registered to receive these votes.

That means there are 20 available classes to be chosen by people who vote.

It also means that, all real votes must be classified within these classes. And they encompass all kinds of political proposals, involving (**pro-democracy electors**) – those who vote for democracy - until (**pro-autocracy electors**) – those who vote for autocracy.

Class Equations

1 - Expressing this in class equations we have that: All electors make up a total of 500 people; so:

$$E - E_1 . \text{Will}_{\text{Electors}} = 500$$

Where: E is the official number of electors classified to vote; E_1 is an objective value introduced in the equation by the imponderable factor; Will $_{Electors}$ is the imponderable factor that represents the will of electors to interfere in the objective equation (active=1; inactive=0).

Electoral equation is a class equation that explains an electoral process. This is the classic form for an electoral equation.

2- Classifying electors according to their attendance to the electoral process we have that:

$$E - E_1 \cdot \text{Will}_{Electors} = V_1 \cdot \text{Will}_{to\ vote} + N_1 \cdot \text{Will}_{not\ to\ vote} = 500.$$

Where: V_1 is the number of elector who cast their votes on Election Day; N_1 is the number of electors that do not go to the polls; Will $_{to\ vote}$ is the imponderable factor that represents the will of those who vote and introduces V_1 into the equation (active=1; inactive=2); Will $_{not\ to\ vote}$ is an imponderable factor that represents the will of those who do not vote and introduces N_1 into the equation (active=1; inactive=0).

3 - Now, classifying voters according to their democratic preferences:

$$V_1 \cdot \text{Will}_{to\ vote} = D_1 \cdot \text{Will}_{for\ Democracy} + A_1 \cdot \text{Will}_{for\ Autocracy}$$

Where: D_1 is the number of electors that prefer a democratic system; A_1 is the number of electors that prefer an autocratic system. Will $_{for\ Autocracy}$ is the imponderable factor that represents the will of those who vote for democracy system principles and introduces D_1 into the equation (active=1; inactive=2); Will $_{for\ Autocracy}$ is a similar imponderable factor.

Then we may write the **electoral equation** this way:

$$D_1 \cdot \text{Will}_{for\ Democracy} + A_1 \cdot \text{Will}_{for\ Autocracy} + N_1 \cdot \text{Will}_{not\ to\ vote} = 500$$

Environment Democracy Indicator

We call: D_1/A_1 = **Environment Democracy Indicator**.

When the **environment democracy indicator** is greater than 1 we may elect a college of representatives that will introduce democratic principles and values on the system. But for that to materialize we need an election that is free and democratic.

A free and democratic election is one where all democratic principles are present in their maximum extent. But in reality some electors may try to impose their will against the will of others.

Activism influence on Electoral Process

Those who want to change other people's will, become themselves, imponderable factors that may introduce value in the **electoral equation**. Their influence may be expressed in class equations like this.

$$\text{Activism} = D_2 \cdot \text{Will}_{\text{Desist Democracy}} + A_2 \cdot \text{Will}_{\text{Desist Autocracy}}$$

Where: D_2 is the number of those who desist to vote for Democracy; A_2 is the number of those who desist to vote for Autocracy; $\text{Will}_{\text{Desist (Democracy or Autocracy)}}$ are imponderable factors that represent the power of activism to change the equation (active=1; inactive=0).

The number of those in activism mood depends on specific conditions of every election. Because of this, the electoral equation now stays like this:

$$D_1 \cdot \text{Will}_{\text{for Democracy}} - D_2 \cdot \text{Will}_{\text{Desist Democracy}} + A_1 \cdot \text{Will}_{\text{for Autocracy}}$$
$$- A_2 \cdot \text{Will}_{\text{Desist Autocracy}} + \text{Absentees Will}_{\text{not to vote}} = 500$$

The activisms of those who favor autocracy reduce the number of those who favor democracy on Election Day. And those who favor democracy reduce the number of those who favor autocracy in the Election Day. Now let us analyze in more detail this electoral equation.

04 Analysis Class (Election Activists)

Subclass (pro-democracy electors)
- They Introduce A_2 into the election equation

They believe in freedom, and do not believe in violence, as a means of personal or collective conquests.

"The domain of an individual of class (for democracy elector) starts and finishes in him". That occurs because sovereignty is equally distributed among all participants; that's why naturally they promote peace.

Class (pro-autocracy electors)
-They Introduce D_2 into the election equation

But in the class **(pro-autocracy electors)**, all is different.

In exact opposition to those who follow democratic principles, they believe in a **strong authority** that may use its **exclusive state power**, to take away some values from others and give freely to themselves, or to somebody else.

"The domain of an individual of class (for autocracy elector) extends until the last one of his subjects". Any new person submitted to an autocratic power is perceived as "an extension of that autocratic power".

Pro-Democracy elector's vulnerability

Precisely because of this, **pro-autocracy electors** may use aggressive means to subdue **pro- democracy electors** and force many of them not to attend elections.

We may conclude that, due to these class characteristics, if there is maximum tension in the electoral process, we have the following relations movements in the electoral equation:

$(D_1 \cdot \text{Will}_{\text{pro-Democracy}} - D_2 \cdot \text{Will}_{\text{Desist Democracy}})$ – tends to zero.

$(A_1 \cdot \text{Will}_{\text{pro-Autocracy}} - A_2 \cdot \text{Will}_{\text{Desist Autocracy}})$ – tends to A_1.

That means many **pro-democracy electors** may not go to the polling stations, in a context of confusion, tension, and violence. While **pro-autocracy electors,** mainly the most radical ones, may indeed increase their number in the same context.

And so being, they may win an election and change the environment's Objective Political Regime (this concept is discussed in the last chapter of this book), even when the **environment democracy indicator** is very strong, simply by adding confusion, tension and violence to the electoral process.

This is called the "**democratic auto destruction syndrome**" that affects all democratic systems, which may be expressed as follows:

"All democratic system carries inside itself, the agents for its own destruction"

Therefore, the right to vote is free and independent but its value is a dependence of all the votes cast in the ballot box on Election Day. However, those who do not vote give away their right to vote to all who vote in a shared fashion. That means in reality, if a pacifist stays home on Election Day and urban war lords win the election; that was their vote.

05 Analysis Class (Business)

Now let us take a look on Class (Business) to understand a very important phenomenon that occurs on it; that is imbalance redistribution.

Class (Profits)

Class (Profit) is a dependence of Class (Sell). Because of this a businessman cannot impose selling to anyone.

Class (Sell)
Class (Sell (Profit))

Dependences of Class (Profit) are:

Class (Profit)
Class (Profit (Net Profit))
Class (Profit (Tax))
Class (Profit (Work))
Class (Profit (Buy)

Let us analyze each of the dependences:

1- Isolating Class (Profit) we perceive that it only occurs where there is willing of Clients. Client may or not concede to it. Its class equation stays like this:

$$P = P_1 - P_2 . \text{Will}_{Client}$$

Where: P is the profit to be realized; P_1 is the disposable profit in last period; P_2 is a value introduced in the equation by the imponderable factor – that may be positive or negative; **Will**$_{Client}$ is an imponderable factor (active = 1; inactive = 0) that represents the will of clients to alter the disposed profit. When the imponderable factor is inactive then $P=P_1$.

2- Isolating Class (Net profit) we observe that it is under control of the businessman.

$$N = N_1 - N_2 . \text{Will}_{Businessman}$$

Where: N is the net profit to be realized; N_1 is the disposable net profit in last period; N_2 is a value introduced in the equation by the imponderable factor – that may be positive or negative; **Will**$_{Businessman}$ is an imponderable factor (active= 1; inactive=0) that represents the will of the businessman to alter the disposed net profit. When the imponderable factor is inactive then $N=N_1$.

3- Isolating Class (Tax), we verify that it depends on the order of government. Its class equation is:

$$T = T_1 - T_2 . \text{Will}_{Government}$$

Where; the meanings of the symbols in this equation are similar to the ones shown above.

4- Isolating Class (Work), we observe that it depends on the will of the workers - they may accept or fight to change its value. This class equation stays lake this:

$$W = W_1 - W_2 . \text{Will}_{Worker}$$

Where; the meanings of the symbols in this equation are similar to the ones shown above.

5- Isolating Class (Buy) we verify that it depends on the will of suppliers. This equation goes like this:

$$B = B_1 - B_2 . \text{Will}_{Supplier}$$

Where; the meanings of the symbols in this equation are similar to the ones shown before them.

So, we have that, each objective number inside the democratic environment is controlled by a social class outside it. The following figure 06 illustrates these thoughts:

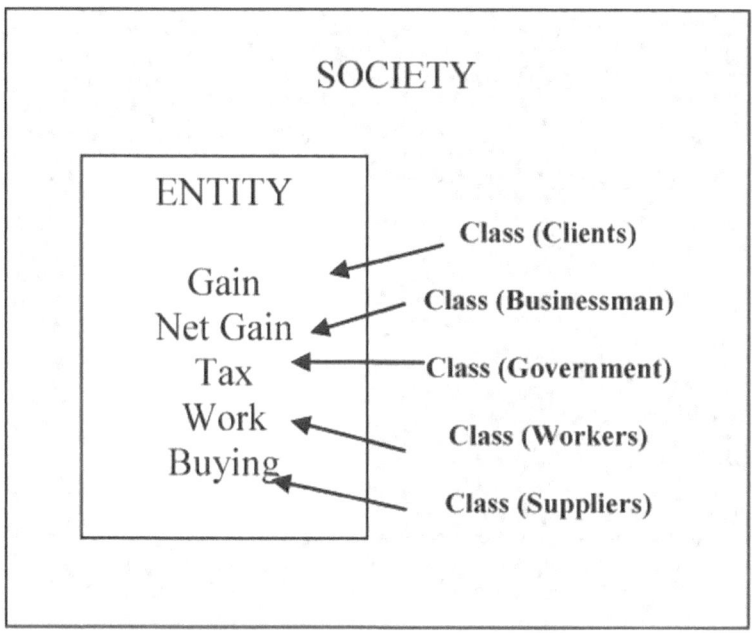

Notice that, if the rule system we are considering is a corporation, or any entity, then government is also part of its society. But we consider government separately because it has exclusive state power and objective rule that are separated from society.

06 Class (Business) Wave

The system of class equations that form an entity class wave is as follows:

(Imbalance =
$P = P_1 - P_2$. $\text{Will}_{\text{Client}}$ +
$N = N_1 - N_2$. $\text{Will}_{\text{Businessman}}$ -
$T = T1 - T_2$. $\text{Will}_{\text{Government}}$ -
$W = W1 - W_2$. $\text{Will}_{\text{Worker}}$ -
$B = B_1 - B_2$. $\text{Will}_{\text{Supplier}}$ -
= 0)

Initially all imponderable factors of this wave are inactive and imbalance is zero.

This wave is balanced, and this system is stable. But when any imponderable factor introduces any real objective value, disequilibrium appears, and needs to be redistributed among the class equations that form the wave, so that the equilibrium may be restored. Which means all imponderable factors may be inactive again.

As you can see for you self, a wave of class equations may easily be confused as a set of simple objective numbers, which has no other ramification beyond them.

And this is exactly the motive why so many professionals around the world commit errors when dealing with these kinds of problems.

Because in reality this wave is constituted by a set of imbalanced equations that subjectively balance themselves with a range of feelings, aspirations, dreams and other emotions from diverse social classes.

Subjective and impersonal Class Equations relate objective democratic value with social, mental, sovereign values. And to each democratic objective value formed, there is a correspondence to a real value that is formed in the day to day dimension of reality.

Therefore, these objective values constitute abstract class objects – which we can see in our calculations - of the real class objects, we see in reality.

That means all in reality is connected, and have a logic explanation to exist. "Reality is too big to resume".

For this reason, class equations allow us to relate our feelings and emotions with reality that we construct in our day to day life.

07 Class (Business) rank

The dependence relation among classes in a class wave, allows us to establish a rank between them. To do this we attribute to the initial class rank 0; to the subclass following in line of dependence we give rank 1; to the next one we rank number 2; and so forth.

Example:

- 0- Class (Businessman's Profit)
- 1- Subclass (Supplier's Profit)
- 2- Subclass (Worker's Salary)
- 3- Subclass (Client's Gain)

This class wave is an abstract class object. A class rank 0 may be realized or not. But classes with greater ranking need to be realized for the wave to exist. That means when we wish to create a certain class object, we need to think and realize all its subclasses. In the contrary we shall be creating a class object that is different from what was thought of. And when we want to destroy a class object, we need to destroy all its subclasses, or we may be creating a class object that is different from what was thought of (or even no class object at all).

Think for a while in the Class (Building (Apartment)). If we decide to construct an "Apartment Building" we have to do from the cleaning of the terrain to the cleaning of the done construction. Including, we also have to construct, foundations, beans, walls, sour system, water system and all sorts of things.

That same thing occurs for all class objects in the real environment. There are many things we need to construct before we may say that our "instantiation job" is done.

Other important thing is that in the democratic-social environment, agents with greater economic power, in principle have more subclasses in their dependence. And agents with less economic power, they have less subclasses in their dependence.

By other side, a real class object belongs to a class, but has a set with an infinite number of precise characteristics. A change in a real object could send it to another class. We may say that this new class has simply substituted the prior one.

Thus, classes resemble labels, added with some characteristics necessary to their existence and the necessary method to form its instance. Be it abstract or real. This method may include all kind of demands in the existential environment (reality plus unreality)

Yet, a class object has identity labels, and values that characterize them. We can realize a class or try to prevent it from materializing using adequate methods.

CHAPTER 4

CLASS LIMITATIONS

In prior chapters we learned that those equations found in the democratic environment, referring to real values, may look like simple set of numbers or objective equations - containing only objective values – but in reality, they carry inside themselves, subjective and impersonal imponderable factors that relate them to feelings, aspirations, wishes, and other sentiments coming from diverse social class agents.

4.1 Puppet Theater Analogy

By analogy we may consider a similar process to this one, what happens in a puppet theater.

Where puppets, made up of wood and other inert materials, develop in stage a performance, as if they were living human being. In reality their human characteristics – like speech and movements – are lent to them by their controllers which stay out of the stage hidden from the audience.

That very phenomenon happens with class equation numbers. Apparently, they look like numbers as any other. But in reality they are subjectively controlled by sentiments, perceptions and other emotions coming from the social classes to which they serve.

In this chapter we will understand class limitations and how disequilibrium distribution occurs inside a wave of class equations.

4.2 Imposed Loss

We call **imposed loss** to a negative imbalance, that appears without our planning and that needs to be paid.

An imposed loss is a bill that needs to be paid. It can happen in any environment, aspect, and dimension of the existence environment.

For instance, we went to play in the rain and got cold; we were aggressive to a friend and lost his friendship; we passed a traffic light and got a ticket; we spoke nonsense and got downhearted.

In nature, in society, in the democratic system the imposed losses occur and always cost us a lot in real value that we have to pay.

The more disciplined that we may be, yet we cannot avoid them to happen because we do not control all class equations of our existence.

But when they occur against us, in the democratic environment, we may pass it on, to someone else's pocket, by using the **value conversion principle**. But when we think of doing just that, we face some **limitations** in the natural, social and rules environment that affect classes and their alterations.

4.3 Class Limitations

Class limitations are out of our will factors, that in themselves do not constitute an imposed loss, but they impede our will to realize. Among these factors we have the following:

1- Class Heritage - Let's consider class (Apartment Building). And we need to create a project out of this class. This means such an abstract class object needs to inherit the characteristics of the Class (Apartment Building). And this abstract class object will correspond to the real class object. That is to say, an apartment building must have the appearance of an apartment building, in reality. If we have any alteration made, in the real class object, then we are creating another abstract class object; that can even belong to other class.

2- Interaction and dependence of a class - So, let's suppose that we are in our apartment and we discover that the kitchen is small. Then we decide to enlarge it. Then we discover that this class change will imply alterations in other classes, like "service area", "rooms", "corridors" and others. Besides, that this change will occur inside the apartment class, from which the "kitchen" is e dependency (subclass).

Thus, an alteration in a subclass may imply alteration in other subclasses, belonging to the same wave of classes, or even to other class waves.

As an example, a reform in our apartment may affect our neighbor's apartment – like spoiling its paint - or affect the building as a whole – such as smashing the common water plump.

That means subclasses always depend and interact with other subclasses.

3- Nature of the class - Important restrictions to class alterations are natural and social or natural, impositions. We cannot alter the basic nature of things. Some alterations may, or may not be, more expensive to be realized due to natural or social limitations.

For instance, a person works for some employer, and wants to find and work for another employer who may offer a better pay. This is a change from a "real work object" to another "real work object", in a higher pay social class. This class alteration may not be undertaken by a person with many sons. But naturally, it may be realized, by a person young single that lives with his parents.

Another example; a 50 years old person cannot be turned into a 10 years old person. And many others.

4 - Class Reference - Some classes have the faculty of being able to use values in other classes as an alternative. For instance, an investor may be informed of interests paid by government to determine the profit he needs to obtain in an investment. Instead, people that live on wage, need to get the information relative to their precise subclass.

The Objective Theory accepts the idea that any "done work" have an intrinsic value that does not depend on the location it is done.

This concept enables us to use the value of work in more efficient environment as an alternative reference. This intrinsic value of work is altered for less by inefficiency of real democratic systems where it is delivered. The class equation for this phenomenon is this:

$$B_R = B - B_2 \cdot \text{System Inefficiency Factor}$$

Where: B_R is the value received in the real system; B is the intrinsic value calculated with consideration to a more efficient system; B_2 is a negative value imposed by the imponderable factor; System Inefficiency Factor is the imponderable factor that, when active, reduces the value of "work done", that is paid to the worker. It represents the inability of the system to pay more efficient value of a "work done".

Notice that in more efficient systems, a "done work" always has a higher value than in inefficient or deficient systems.

We say that the objective factor B_2 constitutes **Free Work** also called systemic difference. That comes to be an imposed loss that is paid by the worker to the employer. It is measured taking into consideration a more efficient value paid out in another system in the very same moment. Because of this, it does not relate to the concept of "depreciation" which takes time into consideration.

5 - Class Domain - One of the most important things with relation to class alteration is class domain. When we speak of class domain, we refer to the power of altering this class or its objects. He, who is able to do so, has the domain over the class.

6 - Class Relation Domain - But class domain alone does not confer the power to alter them. It is needed for that, the domain of all relations with other classes, which may be affected by the alteration.

The Objective Theory accepts the principle that "the power of the weak is a concession of the stronger".

This means he who has the domain over a class and all its relations is going to use it for producing changes that benefit or please him.

For instance, we cannot change the facade of our condominium without approval from the syndic which in turn will only approve it, if that pleases all the condominium participants.

7 - Class Wave Control - A class wave includes many dependent and interactive class equations. We call class wave controller that class that is able to alter or even finish its existence.

A condominium is controlled by its participants collectively.
That means no participant can make alterations not approved by the other participants.

But some types of waves have a class that exerts isolated control over them. A business for instance may be created and finished by its owner at his own will.

Because of this fact we say the owner is the sole controller of the Class (Busyness). As such he may finish one of these waves, and create another anew, even involving new people, products, and clients. For this controller to continue or not in this wave, it is simply an option.

Whenever controllers are facing an imposed loss, they may pass it on to some dependent classes over their domain, or also they may simply close the business class wave, extinguishing in the process all subclasses. This leverage in their power, give them a greater control over alterations in the dependent subclasses. Making the controller able to determine classes, aspects, and values where an imposed loss may rest.

Legislators try to impose on them some legal limit to this class wave control. But it may be exerted in infinite ways including informality.

8 - Power of interactive waves - Other important factor in altering a class, are the interactive waves. Let's consider a person that wishes to ask a salary hike from his boss. But let us consider also that there are many people wishing to change their classes exactly to the position of this person. That means this person may simply be substituted in his position by one of these people that wishes his place before getting any pay hike.

By other side, this person's boss, perceiving an increase in job offer, may use this competitive advantage in favor of his class, to impose against this person a reduction in his work pay.

That means interactive classes that apparently seem to be free in relation to the class waves they interact with; indeed, they have an important relation and may alter them.

This relation occurs in a precedent class that involves them all. For instance in this case, both of these classes – Class (person's position) and Class (other people's position) - are dependent classes of class (work market).

That is precisely the reason why he who lives on his work needs to protect his class from interactive attacks. Not only those coming from democratic-social environment (Disqualification) but also those coming from abroad (Qualitativity). Notice that, Disqualification and Qualitativity are discussed further in this book.

9 - Relative Dependence - it consists of the per centum value to which one class depends on another class. In general, he who has strong dependence submits himself to the will of the other, and the one with less dependency, may control relation between the classes.

For instance, a Class (Supplier' gain) of supplier "S" is formed by 2% in value coming from the Class (Businessman) of businessman "B". We say "S" depends on "B" in a 2% percent value.

Let us consider also that 1.5% of Class (Gain) value of businessman "B", comes from "S". In this case we say that "B" has a relative dependency of 1.5% on "S".

In other example, a worker "W" receives 100% of his monthly pay from businessman "B". But his work contributes only with 1% in net profit for "B". Then we may say that "W" depends on "B" by 100%, and "B" depends on "W" by 1%.

Notice that supplier "S" may interrupt his relation with businessman "B" without significant problems, and vice versa.

But in the case of worker "W" it is evident his vulnerability toward businessman "B".

This means "W" will be an almost certain victim, who will be forced to pay any imposed loss, that threatens the stability of this wave. Hurricane, recession, imbalanced taxation, and violence; anything that imposes loss, presses downward his work pay.

10- Class Risk - When a person roots out a garden plant, probably will not have any additional loss. But if a person lets his car open in the outside in a deficient environment – where "life" means "to find means of survival" – he may not find it when he comes back. **Class Risk** means potential losses relative to dependent class extinction. In this work we evaluate class risk in the form of an addition to the relative dependence per centum.

One car depends on its proprietary. But its loss may include besides itself, other cars dependent of another proprietary; given that both are related by Class (Local traffic).

This means a relative dependence relation for this car and his proprietary is in true much bigger than the one represented by the value of the car itself. To this addition in value of relative dependence we call **class risk.**

In the case of work, the employee's dependence toward an employer may increase significantly as a function of the phenomenon of class risk. The following class equation describes class risk.

Relative Dependency Relation $_{\text{(worker) to (employer)}}$ = D_1 . Dependence $_{\text{Worker}}$ + N x D_2 . Dependence $_{\text{Family}}$

Where: D_1 is the dependence of the worker; N is the number of members of his family under his responsibility; D_2 is their dependency; Dependence (worker, Family) are imponderable factor that represent the will and effect involved (active=1; inactive=0). We may add other parcels to include family members with different dependence rates.

When a worker has wife and children to support, a loss of job may really be dramatic. For a worker with wife and three children that also depend on his wage, the class equation that represents relative dependence is as follows:

Relative Dependency Relation $_{\text{(worker) to (employer)}}$ = 100%. (Worker Dependence) + 4 x 100%. (Family Dependence) = **500%.**

Where: "Worker Dependence" and "Family Dependency" are imponderable factors that are active in this equation (Active=1).

This so extreme vulnerability of work, has taken people all around the world to consider employment as a favor of the employer to the employee, and not **a business relation** as it really is. And at the same time, many governments consider employers as "benefit providers" for workers.

11- Exclusive Estate Power - This is the power that government agents have with exclusivity in the democratic environment, to determine and force people from all social classes by means of "rules", "bars" and "guns"; to do or not to do things.

In "Efficient State" model this exclusive power may only be used to do well to all participants, but in "Just State" model this power may be used to harm, some, many or even all participants, for the benefit of selected others.

CHAPTER 5

IMBALANCE DISTRIBUTION

In this chapter, we shall be studying how an imbalance is redistributed among the classes that form a class wave. Let us consider a wave integrated by five class equations, which are expressed as follows:

(Imbalance =
Class (Gross Profit) "G" +
Subclass (Tax) "T" -
Subclass (Merchandise) "M" -
Subclass (Net Profit) "P" -
Subclass (Work) "W" -
= 0)

We call this a classical expression of a wave, because it shows the classes that integrate the wave. The classes are written within parenthesis, and the class objects they may form are written within quotation marks; but their use may be dismissed, mainly quotation marks. The "Imbalance" object written on top of the wave means the beginning of it. And the last equal sign showing value zero marks the end of the wave.

In order to study imbalance redistribution inside this balanced wave, let us attribute to it some hypothetic values. Let us accept the following values for this wave:

Imbalance =
G = 1000
T = -100
M = -500
P = -200
W = -200
= 0

We call this "objective expression of the wave", because it shows the objects that integrate the wave. As we can see it is balanced and so its imbalance is zero.

Now let's suppose that government has used its exclusive state power and heightened taxation inside this wave in more 100 dollars; making it to be like this:

Imbalance =
G = 1000 +
T = 200 -
M = 500 -
P = 200 -
W = 200 -
= 100 -

Imbalance now is negative. For this reason this class wave becomes active, to internally redistribute this imbalance, until it is stable again.

In order to accompany this redistribution process, in the first place we need to express the **agent classes** that are not expressed in the classic disposition of the wave. This makes it as follows:

Imbalance =
$G = G_1 + G_2$. (Will $_{Clients}$) +
$T = T_1 - T_2$. (Will $_{Government}$) -
$M = M_1 - M_2$. (Will $_{Supplier}$) -
$P = P_1 - P_2$. (Will $_{Businessman}$) -

$$W = W_1 - W_2 \cdot (\text{Will}_{\text{Worker}}) -$$
$$= I$$

So, what seemed to be simple set of disconnected values becomes now a class equation system, each one with its respective objective factor and imponderable factor that controls it.

Where in the class (Tax) we have that: T is the new value after the change; T_1 is the value before the change; T_2 is the value of the change itself; $(\text{Will}_{\text{Government}})$ is an imponderable factor that introduces T_2 and represents will of government (Active=1; Inactive-0) – when it is active it is worth 1 and otherwise is worth zero. In this case it is active. Notice that T_2 may be introduced in the equation with positive or negative value.

After that decision we have now this:

$$T = T_1 - T_2 \cdot (\text{Will}_{\text{Government}}) = -100 - 100 = 200$$

And the wave is as follows:

Imbalance =
$G = 1000 + G_2 \cdot (\text{Will}_{\text{Clients}}) +$
$T = 200 -$
$M = 500 - M_2 \cdot (\text{Will}_{\text{Supplier}}) -$
$P = 200 - P_2 \cdot (\text{Will}_{\text{Businessman}}) -$
$W = 200 - W_2 \cdot (\text{Will}_{\text{Worker}}) -$
$= 100 -$

Imbalance has turned this wave active – that is, all imponderable factors became active - and its agents need to act in order to redistribute this imbalance inside the wave. So that it may be stable again. Someone has to keep this imposed loss. Because of this, all agents defend their attribute classes and eventually pass on to another agent all imposed loss they can avoid. In this moment class limitations appear, some of which, we will examine from now on.

1- Analysis Class (Limitations) - Limitations on imposed loss redistribution

The very nature of the class wave imposes some limitations to all classes of participants in a way that is independent of their will.

This wave considered in this example is a "corporation", and being so, it has a controller. The class that controls it is the Class (Businessman) – the "owner of the company".

As the controller of this wave the businessman may redistribute the imposed loss or simply close the wave – that is, close the company in order to stop it from producing loss. To decide this he must conduct a class analyses in his wave. That is what we are going to do now:

Analyzing Class (Gross Profit) we notice that it is a subclass of Class (Sell). That in its turn is a subclass of Class (Market). As follows:

Class (Market)
Subclass (Sell)
Subclass (Gross Profit)

All this means this businessman may even be put out of business if he tries alone to impose loss against these superior classes. Quite in the contrary they are the ones that may change their dependencies.

Also the businessman cannot change the Class (Tax) because it is under government control, which has the state exclusive power.

Also, the businessman cannot change Class (Merchandise) because it too, is a dependence of Class (Market).

Notice that when there is a change in Class (Market), then all its subclasses also may change, including Subclass (Merchandise). But that is a process over which the businessman has no control.

So, two options are left to him; he must decide to change class (Net profit) that he domains, or he must change Class (Work) he controls through the wave.

If he changes objects in Class (Net Profit) then he is the one to pay the imposed loss. If instead, he changes objects in Class (Work) then he will pass the imposed loss to the workers.

2- Comparison between Classes (Net Profit) and (Work)

Investors

Investors may use Class (Government Interest) or class (International Interest), or other classes as a reference to evaluate the necessary return they must have on a capital investment.

And there is acceptance for their capital investment internationally around the world. So they are relatively free to move it from one country to another if necessary.

These characteristics among others concede them the capacity to recognize any probable losses and defend themselves against them. And that is what they really do all the time.

Workers

Quite in the contrary, workers do not have external references for the value of their work. They count only with information that is supplied by their very employers.

Yet, additionally they operate with high dependence and high risk of losing their jobs.

And all countries with high work value, do not allow invasion of low paid workers coming from inefficient or deficient systems.

Because of that workers do not have international portability for their services.

All this combined make the classes (worker) a very natural candidate to receive and keep, all imposed losses against their class waves. From this, comes the principle of high vulnerability of class (work) expressed as follows:

"All aggression to the democratic environment falls mainly over workers to be paid in the form of imposed losses"

This is the compensation as we shall see later in this book. If there are adequate conditions part of an aggression may be passed on to prices causing inflation.

In accordance to the Objective Theory any work done indeed has an intrinsic value, which is not dependent on place where it is done. This intrinsic value is diminished as a function of the deficiency or inefficiency that exists on the place where it is done.

Because of this, in all democratic systems around the world, workers need protection for their salaries, and also removal of any government aggressiveness that, there may be in the system.

CHAPTER 6

DEMOCRATIC MODE MARKET

In this chapter, we shall use class equations to explain movements in a stock market that functions in a democratic mode. Before this, we shall revise some Objective Democraciology concepts.

5.1 Objective Democraciology Concepts

Rule process – any of various ways one may use, to achieve objectives in a democratic system. They provide the necessary means for interaction to occur between system agents. We classify them as technical or arbitrary processes.

Technical Processes – are those that develop themselves in accordance with a set of logically defined principles. We may foresee their results simple by knowing what is put into them, and also their functioning principles. Also, we may create elaborated methods of analyses to foresee their behavior.

Objective Theory accepts a principle that all democratic systems have objective nature, and technical means of working. Thus, in democratic systems technical processes are predominant.

Rule Market - is a rule construction that allows some participants to offer values in any aspect, and other participants to receive them in exchange for other value in any aspect.

In all markets it is important to find who has the sovereign power over relations, who has the power to execute things, and who has consequent rights over the system. Also it is important to find its class – its conceptual characteristics- its constructor method and methods used to get things done, and what are its results. The figure 07 explains what we are interested to know when analyzing market systems.

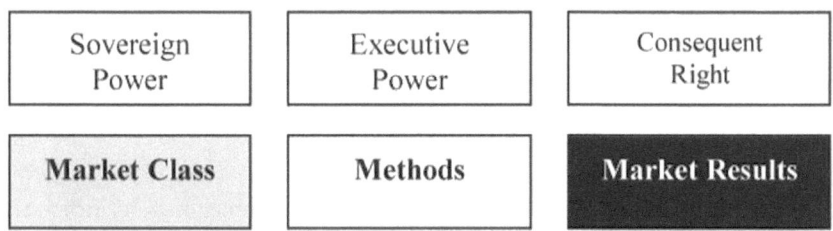

Sovereign power may change object, methods, and class of the market; executive power make things happen; and consequent right accepts market results. "Market Results" is the abstract class object produced in a market class system; for instance, the numbers of the session. Methods are the many ways to have things done in this class, and the way to construct the very market itself. Market Class is the abstract idea from which this market was built and is operating.

Popular (or Participants) Sovereign Decision – is a decision directly determined by the majority of participants in a democratic system. We suppose as being sovereign the decision taken by representatives that have received in ballot boxes, and in their own names, votes from the majority of system participants.

Tuning – is a faculty that processes have, to prioritize the interests of a certain class of people that are interacting through them.

Democratic Tuning – is the faculty that democratic processes have to be tuned with participant's interest.

This means that studying behavior of these classes of participants; we may establish a relation between any present situation and a future result coming from these processes.

Market analysts do exactly this. They make reports of Technical Analyses based on data extracted from market functioning; such as price and volume. Or in other way they make fundamental analyses based upon data coming from corporations that form the market; such as balance sheet and other reports.

5.2 Market Classification

When we say that a market is "democratic" or "autocratic" we are simple attributing to it a **conceptual class** or **label**.

In reality, markets may be formed and may function – as normally occurs - with characteristics that are different from those suggested by their **conceptual labels.**

Objective Theory classifies markets as a function of their formation and operation as follows: Notice that lower level indicate less democratic characteristics, according to LIRA Method of Objective Democratic Evaluation.

According to its formation a market may be:

Democratic Type (or Free) – is formed only by consequent agents (democratic agents).

Government Type (or Restricted) – is formed in part or totally by government agents.

According to its operation a market may be:

Democratic Mode – functions with democratic characteristics – which are known and predefined.

Autocratic Mode – functions without democratic characteristics – they use basic principles which are uncertain and arbitrarily defined.

Mixed Mode (or Multiple) – is formed by different types of markets, or it operates in separate parts with different modes.

In this chapter we shall analyze the **democratic type** and **democratic mode** market.

5.3 Democratic Type Market

Democratic market is one controlled by sovereign decisions taken by its participants.

The fact that there is no isolated authority in sovereign control of these systems, and the way all participants must organize themselves to exert sovereign control on them – what includes the transfer of some functions to systems and authorities – convey to this type of system a predefined, fixed, and above all objective organization. Which one we call Perfect Democratic System.

The figure 8 shows the fixed organization of a democratic system, in any part of the world where they may exist.

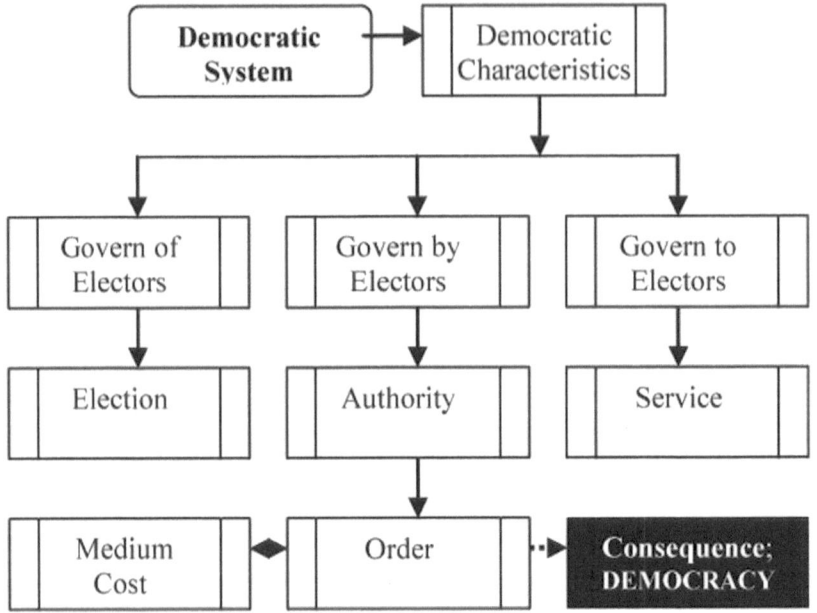

As we see in this flow chart, electors are in control, in administration, and in objective of this type of system. "Democracy" is its abstract class object.

5.4 Conceptual and Actuating Democratic Characteristics

This type of market has a fixed set of characteristics universally known, as **Democratic Characteristics.** There are only 5 conceptual democratic characteristics objectively expressed in the Objective theory, all infinite other are actuating, consequent and day to day characteristics that derive from them.

When anybody chooses this type of system, automatically he also chooses to obey this set of 5 conceptual fixed characteristics - it is not an option.

Without their presence in a democratic system, inevitably infinite syndromes become active and may transform it in a completely different system.

They must be objectively expressed in the official set of rules of any democratic system. And additionally, they must be enforced by actuating agents onto the consequent environment.

The Objective Theory accepts an objective definition for each one of these 5 conceptual characteristics. Those are briefly described as follows:

1. **Popular Sovereignty** - "Participants have the last word about any matter". Popular sovereignty is equally distributed among all participants, who exert it, trough elections. But popular sovereignty in itself does not convey to one, or to a group of participants, the power to command an authority as they wish, without a decision including all the others, in an election.

2. **Freedom** - "Participants are free to take their decisions". Thus freedom characterizes itself by absence of prohibition. Notwithstanding this, freedom exists in the democratic environment along side with other democratic characteristics. That means it is limited by all other characteristics.

    There is a need for the actuating agents to be present in the consequent environment regulating and enforcing the limits on freedom of participants, imposed by all the other principles.

3. **Rule of the Law** (Popular Sovereign Law) - "The actions inside the system are effectively and passively being guided or limited by proper rules". Actuating agents are guiding their actions by the law, and consequent agents as limiting their actions by the law. Observe that the law is elaborated out of the system; then it is voted into the system; where it starts to run as its legal base. It is by principle, a registry of past decisions of participants exerting their sovereignty rights. And the acting agents only regulate and enforce these laws.

4. **Responsibility** - "Each one must pay for the expenses he causes". Thus, nobody is free to take away value from others. Also nobody is free to run away from his or her own responsibility.

5. **Submission** - "Authorities submit themselves to the popular sovereignty and all other democratic principles". This means that an authority do not submit himself to a particular participant, but to all participants collectively. Because of the submission principle, authorities may not violate election result by any means, and a defective election may be replaced by a new election.

5.5 Consequent Democratic Characteristics

The conceptual characteristics form in the consequent environment and consequent dimension infinite consequent democratic characteristics, even after the interference on it of all the others existential environments. The following figure 9 illustrates this thought:

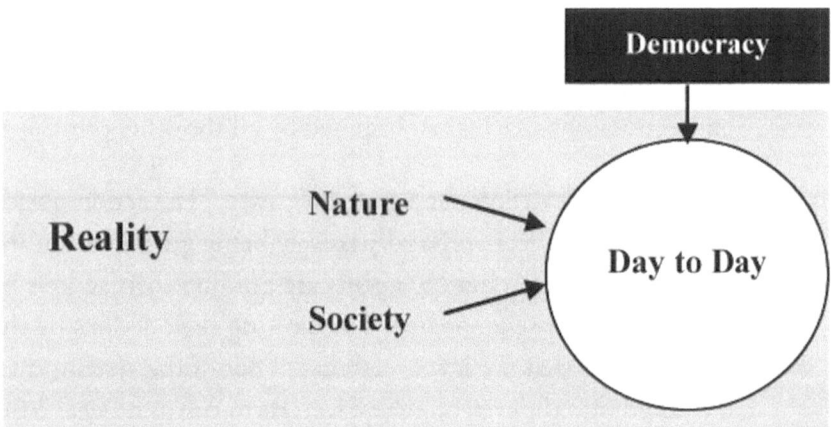

Among all infinite consequent democratic characteristics, there are the ones listed below, which refer to democratic mode operating market.

1. **Objectivity** – the fact that all participants are popular sovereign in a democratic system, and at the same time they have many

other things to do, force these systems to work "automatically". That is, without the constant presence of the popular sovereign. They are officially only present in front of the ballot box at each election. In this case the law and all other characteristics provide the "perfect functioning" of the system. This means these systems function as if they were **machines**, or **objects**.

2. **Referenced Organization** – all democratic systems are formed from one single class that gives its concept, expressed in the following abstract class object:

*"Democracy is the government of the people,
by the people, for the people".*

All democratic systems around the word need to be formed from this same class to be considered a perfect democratic system.

This class defines its characteristics, its objectives, and its methods. "Either you accept democracy or you reject democracy; because you cannot change it".

The **perfect democratic system** has existence in itself independently of human opinion. And it is used as a reference for measuring the presence of democratic principles in real democratic systems that we find in our day to day life.

3. **Common objectives and methods** – all democratic systems ideally have the same objectives and the same methods of functioning. The objectives of these systems are always subclasses of the Class (common good), and their methods are always founded on the democratic characteristics.

4. **Efficiency** – conceptually perfect democratic systems work with maximum efficiency. That means they do not produce imposed losses to their participants.

5.6 Stock Market

A stock market comprehends a set of real values – ownership titles of parts of corporations – that move between persons in reality.

And also comprehends a set of registry that; 1- appear in a computer screen; 2 - increase or decrease at each moment; 3 - and represent on the computer screen, those ownership titles.

These numbers and labels on the screen constitute an "abstract class object", of the Class (Stock Market). They have an identity relation with real values which are moving in real life, and form "real class objects" of this same class.

5.7 Analysis Class (Stock Market)

-Class Relations

Let us analyze Class (Stock Market) in more details:

"Stock market" movements "stock titles", so this is its subclass.

These titles are offered in the market, so "offer" is also its subclass.

"Offer" is formed by "sellers"; so, it is its subclass.

And are demanded in the market; so, "demand", is also its subclass.

Demand is formed by buyers; so, "buyers" is its subclass.

This class relation with their respective ranks stays like this:

    0- Class (Stock Market)
    1- Subclass (Stock titles)
    2- Subclass (Offer)
    3- Subclass (Seller)

2- Subclass (Demand)
3- Subclass (Buyers)

Class (Stock Market) is an option and relates all that is referred to this market.

Subclass (Stock Titles) is a dependency of Class (Stock Market) as a whole, and limits the following subclasses.

Subclass (Offer) is a dependency of Subclass (Stock Titles), it relates all those who are offering stock titles in this market.

Subclass (Sellers) is a dependency of Subclass (Offer) and relates all those who are selling stock titles in this market.

Subclass (Demand) is also a subclass of Class (Stock Titles), and relates all those who are introducing buying requests in this market.

Subclass (Buyers) relates those who are buying stock titles in this market.

"Sellers" and "buyers" constitute an interactive Class (Market Participants).

Initially those in the offer put "sell orders" and those in the demand put "buy orders". These constitute imbalanced waves that change as new orders are entered in the board.

In certain moments appear orders with price that match offer and demand, and equilibrate the market. These businesses are done; these titles are transferred from one owner to the other in other classes; and all data referring to this operation are registered.

As we deal with a market that is located in the Consequent Environment, than we may say that neither the seller are forced to sell, nor the buyers are forced to buy such stock titles.

5.8 Market Behavior

In Democratic Mode

We know that in this kind of market buyers and sellers attend all democratic principles. Which ones, we are not going to repeat in here. So let us analyze some characteristic of a democratic mode of functioning:

8.1 – Market movement democratic mode

Upward Movement

Consider that in a particular day, **a lot more** buyers decide to do business.

That makes business price, and quantity of titles sold, **go up** in such a day.

Consider that in the days that follows movement continues **high** and prices continue to **go up**. Because for example, sellers are profiting from the high demand to receive **more money** for their stock titles.

Demand for the titles may continue to be strong because buyers **expect** to receive more for these titles in the future.

There may be some up or down fluctuations in prices but the mainstream **high** tendency continues firm.

An economy in a **growth cycle** characterizes and justifies this movement.

Downward Movement

Consider that in a particular day; **much less** buyers decide to do business.

That makes business price, and quantity of titles sold, **go down** in such a day.

Consider that in the days that follows movement continues **low** and prices continue to **go down**. Because for example, buyers are profiting of the weak demand to receive **more titles** for their money.

Demand for the titles may continue to be weak because buyers **do not expect** to receive more for these titles in the future.

There may be some upward or downward fluctuations in prices but the mainstream **low** tendency continues firm.

An economy in a **recession cycle** characterizes and justifies this movement.

8.2 – Market Operations Democratic mode

Buy and Sell

When we buy a title in the stock market, we bind a certain amount of our money to that title.

Thus the vendor "catches the money we paid him, and goes away with it" and we "catch the title that we just bought, and come home".

This means that our finance budget is imbalanced.

So, our "decision to buy a stock title" is justifying at this moment this finance imbalance.

Or otherwise, we could say it is classically balancing it.

The Class (Decision to buy a stock title) is balancing the objective value that is missing in our finance budget.

We may express this by the following class equations:

"Decision to buy a stock title" = - 1.000 dollars

Imbalance =
Finance Budget
= - 1.000 dollars

When we diced to sell the title, this "decision to sell" will balance all new receipt, which may include a gain or loss. A loss means an imposed loss because we did not expect it. And a profit means a realized opportunity.

We may express this in class equations as follows:

"Decision to sell" = + (1.000 + R) dollars.

Imbalance =
Finance Budget
= R dollars

Where: R is the operation result

Decision base in a mode democratic market

In their turn, the "decisions to buy or to sell", that we took – and made us assume a loss or win a real profit – based themselves in "our expectations" for the future of the market.

That means each decision to sell or buy in this kind of market is based upon participants own expectations about the future.

This may be expressed as follows:

"Expectations for future result" = "upward"
"Decision to buy" = "yes"

"Expectations for future results" = "downward"
"Decision to sell" = "yes"

Notice that:

1. Participant expectations and decisions constitute separate but interactive waves.

2. Being that, the "expectations=results" wave is integrally formed in the mental environment of participants.

3. And the "decisions=actions" wave is in part formed in the mental environment of participants, but it has other part formed in the objective environment represented by the stock market.

4. One wave interacts with the other changing its value. For instance, an expectation that changes its value may alter a buying decision; from "buy (yes)" to "sell (yes)". One decision that changed its value may alter expectations; for instance from "is going up" to "hope is going up".

5. Thus, simply watching the price balance of a mode democratic market we may know what its participant's expectations are.

6. Based on these expectations we may foresee some of its objective future behavior.

Class equations are meant exactly to balance immeasurable ideas (subjective), with measurable matter (objective) – "thoughts" with "actions".

Where we find one class equation we find many others. Due to the objective and subjective factors successively formed from an alteration of the objective environment. They never appear isolated in life environment..

For instance, any business that is completed in the market involves buyers, sellers, and many other classes not registered here; every one with its respective class equation.

By other side, this anticipation of results faculty of democratic mode markets causes the surge of specialized study areas, concerning various aspects of their present and future behavior.

Also causes the surge of an industry that sells consulting services to their participants. They operate through images, sound, printing and recently, via computer screens. They reach millions or even billions of people around the world.

With the internationalization of knowledge brought about by "globalization", these studies and these industries reach every next day, a greater global audience.

8.3 – Future Value in a Democratic Mode Market

The class equation that relates "future value" with "participants' thoughts" on a democratic mode market may be expressed in the following way:

$$P_F = P_A + V_M \cdot \text{Market Factor}$$

Where: P_F is the expected future price; P_A is the last closing session price; V_M is an objective value introduced in the equation by the imponderable factor; Market Factor is the subjective imponderable factor that represents the intervention of market participants (active = 1; inactive = 0).

If the market is closed then PF = PA, because the subjective factor equals zero.

But if the market is open then the imponderable factor assumes value 1 and an objective value may follow a tendency of thought of the participant's college.

Notwithstanding this, considering the faculty of conformation of value VM, to technical or fundamental patters, we may perfectly use an objective equation as a substitute for the above subjective class equation. Such as follows:

$$P_F = P_A + V$$

Where: P_F expected future price; P_A last closing session price; V is a valor that expresses the variations, we add or diminish to solve the problem.

To estimate the value of this variation we may consider that expectations of participants are stable, and use for instance a medium of closing prices of a certain number of past sessions. Or otherwise we may use more sophisticated formulas of calculations that take into account, many other factors.

Notice That

1. Conceptually in multi investment democratic mode markets that operate in democratic mode, the returns offered, varies as a function of risk, liquidity and security of the investment.

2. For this reason, in more efficient markets the returns offered by stock investments use to pay more returns than government basic rate, and the majority of debt investments.

3. By other side, many imponderable or external factors, in reality affect the behavior of a democratic market compromising its prevision faculty.

4. That is why even in more efficient markets, our calculations about the future will always be just calculated expectations about its future behavior.

5. Furthermore, many deficient or inefficient stock markets obey autocratic models of behavior, some of which we will consider later in this book.

8.4 – Track and Speculators in a Democratic Mode market

All these are logical standards that with others together they govern all democratic mode market.

Under any situation consequent agents are the dominant part in business under this market mode.

Some time buyers do act, and sellers accept consequences, other time sellers do act, and buyers accept consequences.

In order for everything to go well, all democratic characteristics must be present. When this occurs, we say we have e **democratic mode market**.

But these relations between "objective decisions" that are always certain, and "future subjective expectations", that are always uncertain, cause the trajectory of prices in a democratic mode market to be twisty and cyclical. We may assert that in a democratic mode market we go up also "going down", and we go down also "going up". Hence we have the principle:

"The shortest way between two track points in a democratic market is a twisty and cyclical curve"

Speculators

This faculty of having its behavior foreseen brings to a democratic mode market a different class of participant. This is the speculators.

Conceptually, speculators act in a market buying when there is scarce demand, and selling when there is scarce offer.

They win the spread between price paid and price sold. And may not be interested in carrying any of the titles they buy with them.

As they buy titles, they reduce selling pressure on the market and as they sell, they reduce buying pressure on the market.

This way they contribute to a reduction in the twisting of the market trajectory making it more stable and also, they make the longer-range tendencies more evident to all market participants.

For this reason, they are very much welcome in this market mode.

CHAPTER 7

AUTOCRATIC MODE MARKET

In this chapter we shall analyze the behavior of an Autocratic Mode Market, and use class equations to speculate about its movement. Before this we need to revise some Objective Democraciology concepts.

6.1 Objective Democraciology Concepts

Arbitrary Processes – are those where only their controllers know their exact procedures, motivation and results. Controllers are persons who are in charge of determining things in these types of processes.

Objective Theory accepts the principle that all autocratic systems have subjective nature, and arbitrary means of working. Thus, in all autocratic systems arbitrary processes are predominant.

Autocratic Decision - is any decision that do not qualify itself as Popular Sovereignty Decision.

Autocratic Tuning - is the faculty that arbitrary processes have to be tuned with the interests of their controllers.

Their controllers may hire assessors to produce informative reports for them. But nobody is able to foresee their decisions. Autocratic decisions are imponderable factors that introduce objective values in arbitrary processes.

6.2 Autocratic Market

Autocratic Market is one, where sovereign decisions are taken by a single one, or a group of participants. The fact that there is an authority or a group of them in sovereign control of these systems, who are able to set the rules and methods to get things done, as well as the way all its participants must organize themselves to obey their decisions, give such organization an structure that, although arbitrarily formed, may be very light and always centered in the sovereign controller. The following figure 10 shows an autocratic flow chart:

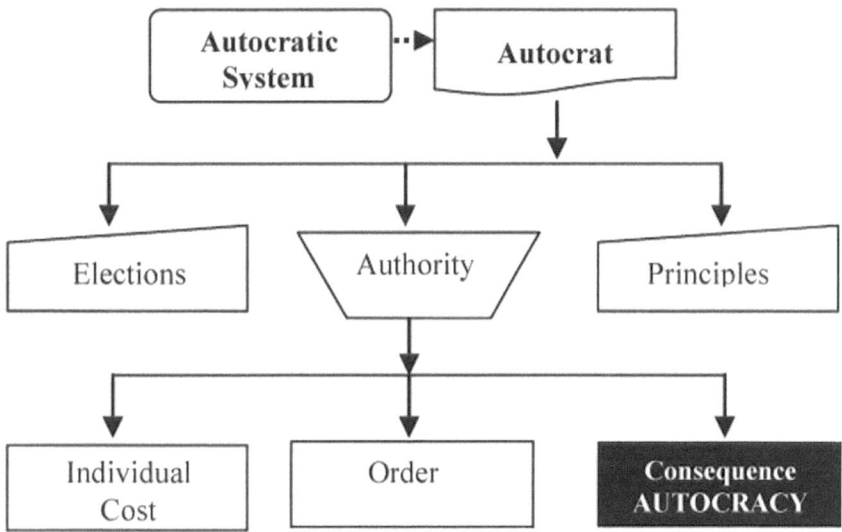

As we may see in this flow chart, autocrats are the ones who govern this kind of system. At their disposal they may have elections, authorities and basic principles – which they regulate, establish their objectives and characteristics, and conduct or limit their results. Elections and principles they may or may not have, but authorities they always have. Authorities make things done in these systems. The consequence of this system is an "Autocracy", which is its abstract class object.

6.3 Conceptual and Acting Autocratic Characteristics

This type of market does not have a fixed set of conceptual objective references. It is a task attributed to their controllers to establish, to maintain and to change the conceptual objective autocratic characteristics - also known as basic principles - of these systems. Each one of these systems has its own set of basic principles. Which ones may be expressed or even hidden within its official set of rules.

6.4 Consequent Autocratic Characteristics

The conceptual basic principles define infinite consequent autocratic characteristics on the consequent environment and consequent dimension, after their interaction with all other existential environments through day to day dimension. The following figure 11 illustrates this thought:

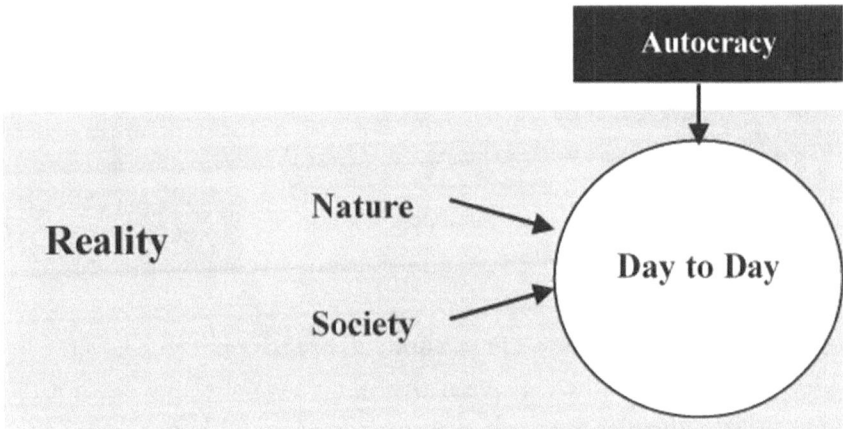

As conceptual basic principles, are established by controllers of the system, than consequent autocratic characteristics are different in every autocratic system. So, each autocratic system is unique. Therefore, some classes of principles are common to all autocratic systems; among them, there are these ones cited as follows:

1. **Subjectivity** – controllers domain these systems and impose on them their styles, and their preferred objectives. And they may use this freedom to create, change, discontinue their basic principles in the moment and by the motivation they wish. – "controller wants"; "artist wishes"; "owner determines".

2. **Subduing** – controllers impose themselves by means of aggressiveness, against all participants and people which they interact with, and think differently. Due to this characteristic, controller's power increases, with the number of participants or non participants, which are, subdued. And because of this, controllers are always reforming the autocratic system in order for it to become more efficient in subduing people. And also they are constantly looking for a greater and more intense domain over an ever growing amount of people.

3. **Aggressiveness** – consists of imbalanced actions that are imposed against participants and subdued nom participants to have them do what is asked by controllers of the autocratic system.

4. **Free organization** – an autocratic system is organized with basic principles which are established without any fixed universal reference – "in them all that is doable may happen".

5. **Autocratic Tuning** – in all autocratic systems, participants and subdued nom participants are conveyed to tune their actions with the will of controllers. These controllers may impose heavy losses against those who do not conform to this class (will of controller).

6. **Objectives and Methods Diversity** – an autocratic system may attend to any objective, and may use any method their controllers wish. Including those that are ethical, unethical, moral, immoral, legal, illegal, expressed or hidden, double, treble, desirable or undesirable, and many other subclasses;

against one, many, or all participants. Conceptually the real objectives of any autocratic system are known only by their controllers.

7. **Inefficiency** – conceptually autocratic systems operate inefficiently with relation to participants. The value of this inefficiency varies as a function of its deviation from the democratic principles. **More Efficient** systems are less inefficient and **Deficient** Systems are more inefficient.

More Efficient System means the great majority of its processes attend democratic principles. **Deficient** System means the great majority of its processes attend autocratic characteristics.

6.5 Corresponding Classes of Autocratic Characteristics

According to the LIRA Method of Democratic evaluation, an opposite concept for each one of the objective democratic characteristics may be used as a kind of "anti-class reference" for autocratic principles as follows:

Conceptual Democratic Characteristics:
Agents' Sovereignty
Agent's Freedom
Authorities' Submission
Responsibility
Rule of the Law

Classes of autocratic Characteristics:

Authorities' Sovereignty
Authorities' Freedom
Agents' Submission
Irresponsibility
Rule of Authorities' Decision

Notice that Democratic characteristics are objects while autocratic characteristics are classes. Through this classification we may evaluate each considered basic principle with relation to the objective democratic principle that generates its opposite class. For instance, if in a certain system; 40% of public value is being transferred to those who did not pay then we have 40% of government irresponsibility in that aspect.

6.6 Analyses of Class (Inefficiency) Cost

Inefficiency – are, costs formed by values that are lost by classes of participants, due to undesired occurrences. They may occur in all existential environments – reality plus unreality. In this text we classify these costs as:

I- Internal Cost (within the rules environment)
II- External Costs (within Society, Nature or both Environments)
III- Imponderable Cost (within Mind, Sovereign or both environments)

Let us analyze these classes in detail:

6.7 Internal Cost

Internal Cost consists in a value that is paid to the system, but not received back by he who paid. The values received by controllers in this class of internal cost may found any different of "common good" objective. Notice that "common good" is good things to all and every one of the participants of a system. We say that internal costs fund all internal losses in a system.

We may identify some classes of internal costs; such as follows:

1. **Autocratic Decision Cost** – this cost surges because any autocratic decision is based upon **"supposition"** that the client will decide in a certain moment, direction, sense, and intensity.

They are not based upon the real client's decision. Exactly in the difference between the "supposed decision" and the effective real "client's decision", resides the cost of autocratic decision. The greater may be the tune of an autocratic decision with the client's will, the lesser may be this cost. Therefore, investors have created a "defensive philosophy" that consists in the orientation of their business toward the will of their client. Through that they identify client's preferences to help controllers decide and operate their autocratic systems with more efficiency. Notwithstanding this, in government systems, state exclusive power may be used to force participants to accept undesired decisions. Then, a decision cost converts itself in repression cost.

2. **Submission Costs** – Consists on resources exclusively mobilized to submit people to the will of controllers. They may assume the form of Repression, Misleading, Censorship, Concealing, and others. **Repression** consists on mobilization of recourses to force someone to accept a loss. **Misleading** consists on mobilization of recourses to induce someone to accept a loss. **Censoring** it is an official ban on certain information flow. **Concealing** is an informal ban on certain information flow. Government systems use "exclusive estate power" for repression and censorship. Market systems use "market power" for misleading and concealing. Notice that Enforcement is simply a cost of providing a service to someone who paid.

3. **Waste Cost** – these are losses that occur in autocratic systems mainly related to the absence of democratic principles.

We may destroy value using a variety of means and employing a small sum of resources. For example; there are many ways to destroy "some one's reputation"; or one may destroy "a house", in many different ways. While value construction occurs only when we use a restricted set of means and we employ a high sum of resources. For example; there are few and hard ways to build "a commercial brand"; or it costs dearly and demand a precise technology to build "a house". Absence of responsibility creates a proper environment for value destruction to occur in an accelerated way because people are unable to relate what they pay, with what they or other agent classes receive back.

Repression and **waste cost** may end up been accounted as simple enforcement of "regular law", and this way they may remain hidden in the system.

Considering all that was said here, we may conclude that, internal cost in aggressive autocratic systems may continue to expand forever without stopping.

6.8 External Cost

External costs are costs paid by autocratic systems participants by means of compensation, due to aggressive actions of their systems against other environments.

To better understand the idea of external cost, let us consider the following analogy:

Citizen A, noticed that his neighbor N, used to wake up late in the morning every day. So he citizen A, decided to wake him up earlier every day – to make him "profit more of the day".

To realize this, citizen A bought a percussion instrument and would position himself in front of his neighbor's house early in the morning every day. And would make noise, until he could see his neighbor N, walking around, inside his home. Thus in reality we have that, citizen A spent some of his money with an instrument he did not need, and was simple losing some of his time every day bothering his neighbor N.

But his neighbor N, due to the aggressiveness of citizen A, had to sleep early every night; and because of this, he had to give up doing what he was used to do - in order to wake up early every day. Then, neighbor N hired an attorney to stop via judicial system the aggression of citizen A. The value neighbor N lost due to the aggression of citizen A, constitutes an **imposed loss** that he wishes to receive back via the judicial system. And that may end up being paid by the aggressive system of citizen A in the form of external cost.

6.9 Imbalance Waves

The set formed by an imbalanced action with its respective reaction constitutes an imbalance wave.

Notice what happened in the described analogy:

a - The noisy behavior of citizen A in his proper rule system was countered by judicial system reaction of neighbor N in **society environment of citizen A.**

b - By the side of neighbor N we have that; the losses he suffered because of the aggression in his rule system, are countered by **judicial system compensation gain** he obtains in **his society environment**.

c - And each imbalance wave carries objective factors that cause the formation of new subjective factors, which in turn create new interactive imbalance waves. Example; citizen A's attorney counters neighbor N attorney; there are now things that citizen A left undone and there are things that were realized in his system, with or even without his desire to.

d - If we consider that citizen A, and neighbor N, live in the same government system, then we may say that these imbalanced waves occurred in the very democratic system.

Through this we may say that: "Any imbalance we impose against the democratic environment causes an infinite number of other imbalance waves which propagates throughout the entire democratic environment".

We call this the **principle of propagation of democratic imbalance.** Imbalance waves propagate themselves in a democratic system exactly as a stone that we have thrown in the surface of a lake, creates waves that propagate themselves throughout the entire lake – as shown in figure 3.

6.10 Imbalance Analysis

Before we discuss imbalance analysis, let us understand how Objective Theory classifies Social Actions done by a Government System, which is the following:

1. **"Civilism"** – constitute day to day actions to defend, preserve and foster democratic and other ethical principles and values.

2. **"Solidarity"** – constitutes actions to collect tax from those who constitute a majority in a government system and then, diliver it, by any means, to a minority that are in need, in order to elevate the utility of the system for all its participants.

3. **"Fraternity"** – constitutes actions to dispose an account to those who want to, to pay donations that are delivered to those who are in need.

4. **"Support"** - constitutes actions to collect tax from those who are selected to pay, by enforced law against their will; and deliver it to those who are selected to receive. This constitutes a system aggression against society.

Notice that higher level means less democratic characteristics – or further away, if you prefer.

1.0 – System aggression against society

System aggression against society causes the appearance in the democratic system of two imbalanced proper rule agent classes that are; **Supporter** and **Supported**. And three classes of proper rule fluxes;

they are **Imbalanced Tax**, **Repression** and **Subsidy**. Let us know a little more about them:

1.0 – Proper Rule Imbalance Agents (two classes)

1.1 – Supporter – is a democratic agent that pays imbalanced tax.

1.2 – Supported – is a democratic agent that receives **Subsidy**. A supported may be personal or corporative. **Personal Supported,** are those who receive subsidy as a means of living. They may use it as a substitute for **Solidarity** or **Fraternity**. **Corporative Supported,** are those who receive subsidy for corporative reasons. They may use it as a means of bail out, or investment, or corporate expansion, including abroad.

2.0 - Proper Rule Imbalanced Fluxes (three classes)

2.1- "Imbalanced Tax"

Is a tax paid to government without any corresponding return to the payer. It is an **objective imposed loss** against the **Supporter** that reaches a **percent** of his social gain.

This means for every dollar that is collected as imbalanced tax, it is necessary to allow a greater amount of dollars to be kept by the Supporter. In other words; "the more a Supporter pays in imbalanced tax, the more he earns in profits"

Also imbalanced taxes are paid to government authorities, that decide who will receive it as subsidy. That tells us nobody can say precisely where the money goes. It may go to those in need, or to those who want simply some free money. Imbalanced tax is also called "**over-taxation**";

2.2- "Repression" consists on mobilization of recourses to force someone to accept a loss.

2.3- Subsidy is an objective gain for the Supported that is regulated and paid by authorities that control a system. It is not possible for the Supported to receive more money or value than he is entitled to receive, in the program.

We call **"Support"** to the sum of Repression plus Subsidy- because it is necessary repression to force the payment to occur:

Imbalanced Tax = Repression + Subsidy

And we call "Support System" to the one that supplies support

II - Society interactive response to system aggression

System aggression against society causes the appearance in society of tree social agent classes; that are **compensation receiver**, **compensation trader** and **compensation payer**. Also appear in society four social fluxes classes, which are; **compensation**, **compensation gain**, **compensation payment**, and **compensation stock**. Let us know a little more about them:

3 – Interactive social agents (three classes)

3.1 - Compensation Receivers are participants or nom participants that receive **compensation**.

3.2 - Compensation Traders are those participants or nom participants who transport compensation without receiving it. Their objective is passing it on to another **trader** or to a **receiver**.

3.3 - Compensation Payers are those participants of the aggressive autocratic system that pay **compensation**.

4 – Interactive social fluxes (four classes)

4.1- Compensation is a value that is subtracted or added to market price of a work done, a service supplied or a product in a way that **favors the receiver**. The following are some of its characteristic:

a- It is calculated taking into consideration intrinsic value of things, in a more efficient market.

b- It may be expressed as a not paid or paid in excess, value relative to a work, service or product. Also it may be expressed as an amount of free work, service or product that has to be offered in order to be received the value of a single unit paid in a more efficient price.

c- It is a "class-imposed loss" that reaches all objects of the classes affected.

d- It is imposed even on those who did not ask or receive any government subsidy at all. A child is already born with the compromise to pay compensation on his work, services or products. We say that it has the same nature as **Christian Original Sin; we are born with that obligation.**

e- It compromises a fraction of the payment someone receives. That means **"the more compensation someone pays the less payment he receives"**.

f- It is paid mostly to the employer, or the consumer. That means its beneficiaries are very well known, and they are not in needy.

For instance; if a product is offered in the market for 7 dollars, but is worth 20 dollars in a more efficient market; in this case there is 13 dollars compensation in that market price.

4.2- **Compensation Payment** is a compensation that is delivered to someone.

For instance; if someone delivers that product cited above, he pays 13 dollars in compensation payment for each unit he supplies.

4.3 - **Compensation Gain** is a compensation that is obtained by someone. We may say that it is a value not paid or gained in excess by the receiver of the work, service or product. The following are some of its characteristic:

- a- **Class (Compensation Gain)** is a social gain for Class (Supporter), that is received in society from the **Class (Compensation Payer).**

- b- The possibility of receiving it is determined only by the style, capability, and decision to profit from the opportunity, taken by the **compensation receiver** or **compensation trader**.

- c- There are no limits for the amount received in **Compensation Gain**. For instance, a home or company owner may have as many employees as they desire to; each of them generating **Compensation Gain**. This means Supporters may materialize as many "**Compensation Gain Objects**" as they wish and are able to.

- d- Because of this, a **Compensation Gain** may be composed only by **Advantage** to the receiver.

For instance, in the same example above, the buyer of such product gets 13 dollars in compensation payment for each unit he buys.

4.4- **Compensation Stock** is a compensation that is being transported in some work, service or product.

For instance, still in the same example cited above, if the buyer is not the final consumer of that service, then he maintains those 13 dollars in compensation stock to sell later to someone else.

Notice that compensation behaves like the commodity it is in. And likewise, they may be sold to trader, exported, or liquidated.

But all these phenomena exist only in the scope of the Objective Theory, which considers the existence of an external more efficient or perfect reference for values in real democratic systems.

8.4 Support Waves

Support occurs when someone takes value away from one person, without his will and using superior power, and delivers it to another person. It may be illegally, informally or governmentally practiced. Whenever a government engages in Support practice, authorities use their exclusive state power to take money or other values, away from some agents in a democratic class called Supporter; and deliver it to other agents in a class called Supported. As these democratic classes are chosen taking into consideration their corresponding social classes, we may say it deals with **forced value transference** among social classes. This is a classical example of external aggressiveness that creates fluxes, which in their turn, form waves as follows:

8.4.1 - Class Wave (Support)

Imbalance =
Imbalanced Tax +
Repression -
Subsidy -
= 0

The following figure 12 illustrates a **Support** wave:

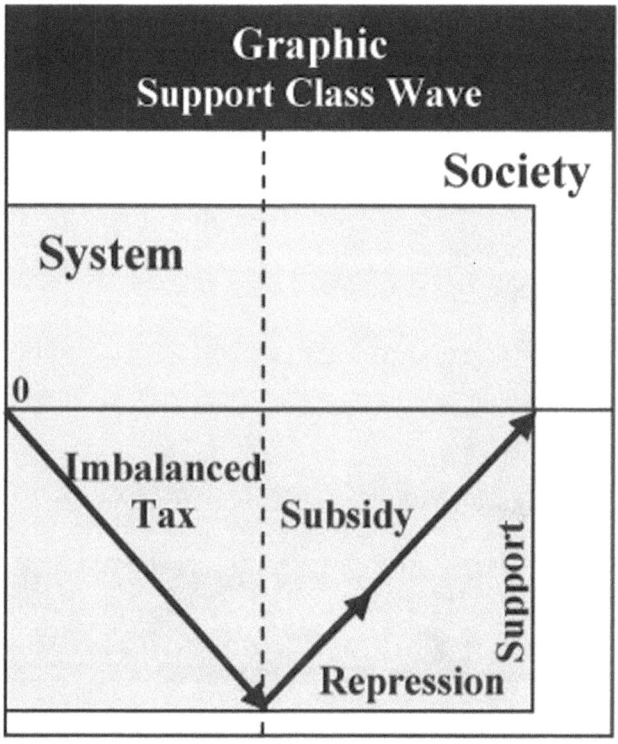

This class wave is formed inside the democratic environment and balanced according to the will and power of system controllers.

8.4.2- Imbalance Wave (Compensation Gain)

But **Supporter** becomes **Compensation Receiver** in Society. Where he uses his market power to differentiate values he pays for work, service and products that he buys, in order to compensate himself for the values he lost to the aggressive government system. Therefore a **compensation gain** wave is formed, according to the following:

A- In the first leg we have the **Imbalanced Tax** paid to the aggressive government, and **disadvantage**. **Disadvantage** is a social cost that is added to the cost of the aggressiveness relative to its processing or other implication. For instance; cost of accounting, risk, or security etc.

B- And in the second leg we have the **Compensation** and an excess value that we call **advantage**; together they form **Compensation Gain**. **Advantage** is a part of Compensation Gain that does not correspond to any prior payment to the government. The wave is as follows:

Imbalance =
Compensation Gain +
Imbalanced Tax −
Disadvantage −
Advantage −
= 0

The following figure 13 illustrates a **Compensation Gain** wave:

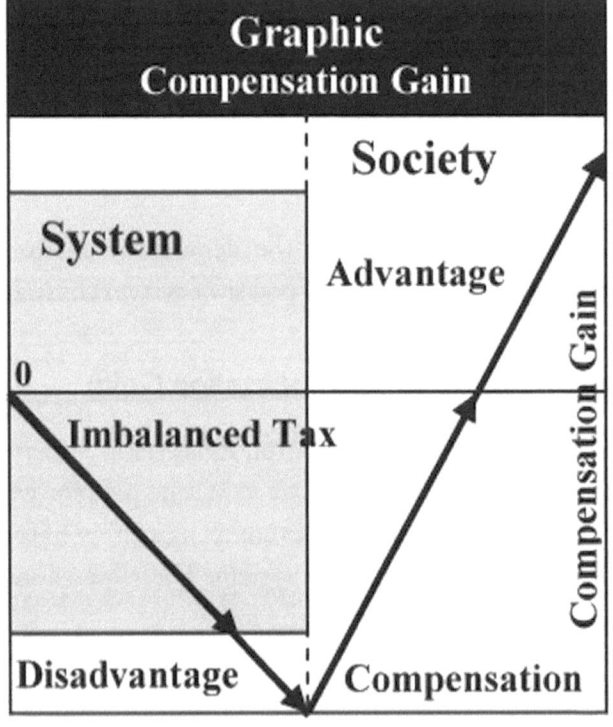

Numerical example of **Compensation Gain** wave:

Consider one person has paid 1.000 dollars less for a certain service. But has paid Imbalanced Tax in the amount of 400 dollars, and has paid to an accountant, 20 dollars to process this payment. This wave stays like this:

Imbalance =
Compensation Gain = 1.000 +
Imbalanced Tax = 400 -
Disadvantage = 20 -
Advantage = 580 -
= 0

As a result of compensation wave this Support program has returned 580 dollars net to the **Supporter**.

8.4.3- Imbalance Wave (Compensation Payment)

As the **Supporter** becomes **Compensation Receiver**, by means of his market power, he automatically forces the **Personal Supported** to become **Compensation Payer** at the same time.

And the **compensation payment** wave is also formed, having:

A- In the first leg the **Subsidy** received from the aggressive government. For instance, money, school classes, meals, security, or medical assistance that were received.

B – In the second leg we have **Compensation** and a **Difference**; together they form **Compensation Payment**. **Difference** is the difference between the **Compensation Payment** that is paid to the market and the **Subsidy** that was received.

And the **Compensation Payment** wave stays like this:

Imbalance =
Subsidy +

Difference +
Compensation Payment −
= 0

The following figure 14 illustrates this wave:

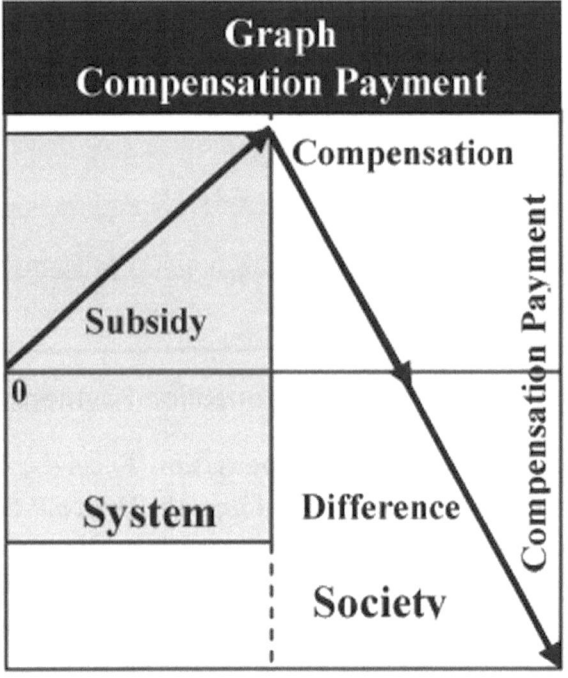

**Numerical example of
Compensation Payment wave:**

Consider one person received 1.500 dollars in value, services and products, "free" of charge from government for his personal use. But this same person is receiving only 400 dollars for his work that fetches 3.500 dollars in a more efficient system. In this case, this person is paying a Compensation of 3.100 dollars and the compensation wave goes like this:

Imbalance =
Subsidy = 1.500 +

Difference = 1.600 +
Compensation Payment = 3.100 –
= 0

As a result of **Compensation Payment** wave this Support program has cost 1.600 dollars net to the Personal **Supported**.

That tells us these support system programs are very deficient in transferring values to the weak. Indeed they take value away from them.

09 Imponderable Cost

Imponderable cost is an imposed loss, or an opportunity lost, that occur because of other costs, and that cannot be classified as internal or external cost.

Analogy

For better understanding of this concept consider the following hypothetic example:

In a certain geographic region there are two countries with democratic system A and democratic system B side by side but with different levels of democratic characteristics.

System A – is democratically deficient.
It is a tough dictatorship where we find people starving; sickness is rampant; and cost of government and its repression are huge.

System B is democratically more efficient.

There, we find people in a much better situation, living a happier life.

The **differences** between system **B** and **A** in any aspect and time, correspond to **internal** and **external costs** of system **A** – which is **deficient**.

Therefore situation in system **B** conveys to its participants certain important gains that are not possible in system **A**.

For instance, people in system **B** are able to **travel around the world**, they may save money and receive **monthly dividends**, and they may **retire earlier.** Nothing of that can be done in system **A**;

So, all that people in system **B** may do and people in system **A** are not able to do, constitutes imponderable cost of system **A.**

How much is the cost of; a lost retirement; a lost travel, and a lost monthly dividend? We know that they are immense, but we cannot measure them precisely. That is exactly why they are imponderable.

10 Imponderable Cost Classes

We may classify imponderable costs according to infinite aspects. In this text we analyze the following classes; **Personal**; **Public**; **Immediate**; **Future**; **Against Participants**; **Against nom Participants**.

Personal – corresponds to all that people cannot do, because of system inefficiency or deficiency. Example: one person who works in a deficient system may not be able to travel in his vocation as easily as a more efficient system participant may do.

Public – corresponds to all a system cannot offer because it operates with a certain level of inefficiency. Because of this, many gifted people simple go out of deficient systems because they cause loss to them. And many imaginative people are forced to follow through the will of controllers and because of this, do not operate well or worse, turn to violence to try to attend their wishes.

Immediate – corresponds to costs due to inefficiency that are being incurred and paid when they are **accounted for**. Example a default or non engagement fine that must be paid immediately.

Future – corresponds to all costs, due to inefficiency, that **will have to be paid** in the future by the actual or future participants. Example; when we have an increase in government debt, without any increase in government revenue. Because nobody knows what should be left undone in the future in order to pay this.

Against Participants – correspond to costs due to inefficiency, to be entirely paid by actual ore future participants. Example; when we have a tax increase; when we have censorship hampering electors decisions; when we have autocratic decisions that need to be overturned on election day, and when we have selective differential processes in course.

Imponderable costs against participants, yet never accounted for, are an important, if not the most important, source of systemic differentiation.

They work in the democratic system the same way, "body tension" works in humans; that is, "they may kill the patient without giving any warning signal". Imponderable costs against participants may destroy most of the values in all democratic system aspects even without being ever noticed.

Against nom Participants – corresponds to all costs due to inefficiencies that exist in another system but is passed on to be paid by the considered system participants.

Example; when participants, merchandise, services, products and work coming from a **deficient system** that legally or illegally enters a more efficient system, with differentiated minor price, forcing down all other prices in this new market via **Qualitativity**.

This way they impose losses to participants of this other system through reduction in their paychecks and reduction in the level of employment in the region.

Notice that:

a- Objective costs may become imponderable costs through censorship and concealing. People simply do not perceive them. For example, in an electoral run, censorship may hide compensation from those who are paying it, making it an imponderable cost unseen by them.

b- Compensations on low prices of work, service and products, generally are not accounted. For example, a "value not paid" in a "work done" as a function of compensation payment, is not accounted, nor registered in any way.

c- Additional values paid as a function of compensation payment may be accounted as unforeseen costs, or normal operation costs. Examples, environmental fine may be registered as incidental cost; additional interest may be accounted as normal operations cost.

d- This miss of accountability for compensations, may cause this cost to continue rising permanently in **deficient systems**. Its imposed losses may reach an ever growing amount of people with an ever greater intensity. That even might be unaware, of the immense problem this cost represents.

e- The limit for internal costs plus external costs corresponds to all public resources in the system. And there is no limit for imponderable costs that may reach all that is yet to be earned by participants. But the natural order of things shows us that as inefficiency cost gets higher and approaches all public resources, an urban war is installed in the system, and government exclusive power is put in a dispute among various different groups that also want to control the system.

11 Autocratic Mode Market

A market is operating under **autocratic mode** when there is a clear definition of a controller. That controller may be one, or a group of authorities, a minority, or a majority of consequent agents. Let us know some of this operating mode's characteristics.

1- Future value in autocratic operating mode

The class equation that relates future value with the will of autocratic market mode controller is this:

$$P_{Future} = P_{Actual} + C . Will_{Controller}$$

Where: P_{Future} is the expected price in the future; P_{Actual} is the price in the last section of the market; C is an objective value introduced by the imponderable factor; $Will_{Controller}$ is an imponderable factor that represents the subjective will of controllers (active= 1; inactive=0)

2- Analysis of autocratic operating mode

2.1 - Controller Will

An operating autocratic mode system follows characteristics determined by its controllers. That means only its controllers can explain its way. Also means we are not able to do so.

By other side we may know its controller and use this knowledge to try to identify the Class (Result). This is naturally a subclass of Class (Controller wishes).

For instance, if the system controller is a group of authorities that act in their own behalf; than that is the way results are coming. If a group of Supported agents controls the system through their votes, results will go in their favor. If a group of people control a system with non identified intention, this non identified intention is its Class (Result).

2.2 - Limits

Variable C follows the decisions system controllers are taking along the way. As a consequence, P Future may assume any value at any moment according to the will of controllers. But the will of controller is limited by his own polices and disposable means to realize it. We may find clues about these limits in the legal base, or set of rules or in the context where the autocratic system is inserted. On informal systems these limits may exist only in the mind of their very controllers.

2.3 - Characteristics Confrontation

Centralized control over autocratic systems that operate receiving and delivering values from and to different social classes causes a **characteristics confrontation syndrome**. Under this syndrome attributes of the classes involved in the operation, may enter in confrontation.

For instance, participants in these systems open their wallets and pay with money they have earned themselves. While authorities simply sign a piece of paper to give the money away to those people they wish, and it is done. That means in reality we may find authorities signing up deliveries of money each time higher even to people that do not pay, and payers just struggling to keep up with payments of these expenses.

To minimize the effects of that syndrome it is necessary that we establish a fixed external reference, with appropriate rule and limitation for these systems. That is; it needs to work as a subclass of a controlled class; in a kind of "controlled decontrol".

CHAPTER 8

MIXED INFLUENCED MODE MARKET

01 Mode Harmonization

A democratic market that operates in democratic mode follows a known set of fixed characteristics.

An autocratic market that works in autocratic mode follows a set of characteristics established by its controller.

These two different sets of characteristics do not blend themselves with each other.

Therefore each one of them keep their separate identity from the other; and causes infinite consequent characteristics.

That means when markets are operating in these two different operating modes in a same bigger market, their infinite characteristics need to harmonize themselves with each other to form a third set of infinite characteristics; that define a mixed market. A mixed market operating mode has characteristics that are very much different from patters of pure democratic or autocratic operating mode. In this chapter we shall discuss a little more about mixed markets.

02 Mixed Mode Market

Government markets, which work in autocratic mode, and democratic markets, which work in democratic or autocratic mode, combine themselves in markets we find in reality forming mixed markets.

If we consider the whole democratic environment as a big market, it works in mixed mode.

03 Mixed Mode Market Classes

We may classify mixed markets as follows:

3- Influenced
2- Manipulated
1- Controlled

Influenced – it is one market preponderantly democratic mode where also there are one autocratic mode market working.

Manipulated – it is one market preponderantly autocratic mode where also there are one democratic mode market working.

Controlled – it is a market preponderantly formed by several autocratic mode markets.

In this chapter we will discuss a few things about mixed influenced and manipulated markets.

04 Influenced Mixed Mode Market

A classic case of influenced mixed market is a government company stock market that works inside a general democratic company's stock market that is much bigger.

Objectively there is no difference among government company stock market and democratic company stock market.

In any case, all goes as described in democratic market chapter.

That means numbers and labels in the computer screen constitute an abstract class object of Class (Stock Market).

They keep an identity relation with values that move in real life and constitute the "real class object" of the Class (Stock Market)

But let us take a closer look into this.

05 Class analyses of mode mixed influenced market

5.1- Class Relation

So we have that Class (Government Stock Market) works as a subclass of Class (Stock market).

And we have that Class (Democratic Stock Market) works as a subclass of Class (Stock Market).

Both of these markets moves "stock titles" so Class (Stock Title), is a subclass of those classes of specific markets – democratic and autocratic.

These "stock titles" are offered in the market so Class (Offer) is a subclass of Class (Stock Title).

Some of these "offers" are sold by "sellers" so Class (Seller) is a subclass of Class (Offer).

These stock titles also are demanded in the market so Class (Demand) is a subclass of Class (Stock Title).

Some of these "demands" are bought by "buyers" so Class (Buyer) is a subclass of Class (Demand).

This class relation stays like this:

0- Class (Stock Market)
1- Subclass (Democratic Stock Market)
1- Subclass (Autocratic Stock Market)

2- Subclass (Stock Titles)

3- Subclass (Offer)
4- Subclass (Sellers)

3- Subclass (Demand)
4- Subclass (Buyers)

Notice that subclasses 2 to 4 are commons to subclass 1. This means there is no difference in business with these titles with respect to type of market.

5.2 – Class Market Analysis

Control

The democratic stock market is formed by many companies that are controlled by many stock holders that aim to obtain profit.

The government stock market is formed by one or, some companies that are controlled by one single controller that is also controller of the government system as a whole.

Their characteristics follow the characteristics of the very autocratic government that controls them.

The Objective Theory accepts that government authorities:

a- Work as a single unit.
b- Have exclusive State Power
c- Do not aim profit

And autocratic governments:

d- Use "Just State Model" – that briefly means they do not observe a relation one to one with respect to right and obligation.

e- Work making deficits in their general accounts.

Rank

The control rank in government company market stays like this:

0- Class (Government)
1- Class (Government Companies)
2- Class (Government Companies Stock Market)

Therefore considering these characteristics we may say that, government companies are managed in accordance to specific official polices, but that are integrated with government policy as a whole.

Behavior of influenced mix mode markets

Notice that we are considering in this explanation, the case of a government market inside a much bigger democratic market as a whole. As a government market constitutes an autocratic allocation of resources, the centralized command will try to impose his will in the direction it takes, and consequently in the track record it produces. By doing this, the autocratic controller affects the market as a whole. Its influence may occur by the infinite forms a common person may use to control his own business. But with an important difference; government company controllers have access to exclusive state power. This means they may produce or have produced rules, politics, practices, doctrines, and do other imposing things that will affect all market as a whole. Also, in a **confrontation of characteristics** with any part of the market, the government is certainly the winner; because, he may function producing losses, while no part of the market can do this. This means government may decide everything about his actuation in any market, even going as "simple businessman"; which definitely he is not. Because of this, these influenced markets show phases in their track record instead of market movements. And these phases are dictated exactly by the autocratic influence they may be receiving. The greater the presence of government market, the greater may be the visibility of these phases in the market as a whole. We show you these phases as we go on.

Growth Phase

In this phase authorities have decided to grow their own market or even the market as a whole. And apply resources and attention to the market to get this done.

They may pay losses or more dividends, reach more clients, buy or incorporate in any way, other businesses, or even take a whole market sector, or a whole industry.

Reduction Phase

In a reduction faze authorities are scaling back their businesses, in value, in clients, in return, profit, in quality or any other aspect they decide.

They may auction some parts or all their business; allow their competitors to take over their market share; or simply abandon their businesses. And the whole market may or may not follow this movement.

5.3 – Future Value of influenced mixed mode market

5.3.1 - Prices used in this text

Market value may be obtained, in different classes. Each of them produces a different value because they take into consideration different set of aspects out of their infinite coordinates. In this text we shall use the following classes:

1. **Substantial Value** – corresponds to the lesser value we obtain selling the considered object or all its parts.

2. **Fundamental Value** - corresponds to that obtained through fundamental analysis – relative to profit, assets, markets and all else.

3. **Technical Value** – corresponds to those obtained by technical analysis – these are studies relative to prices and volume fluctuations in the proper market.

4. **Market, Current, or Actual Value** – correspond to value by which operations are being realized in a market at a given time.

Figure 15 below illustrates this thought:

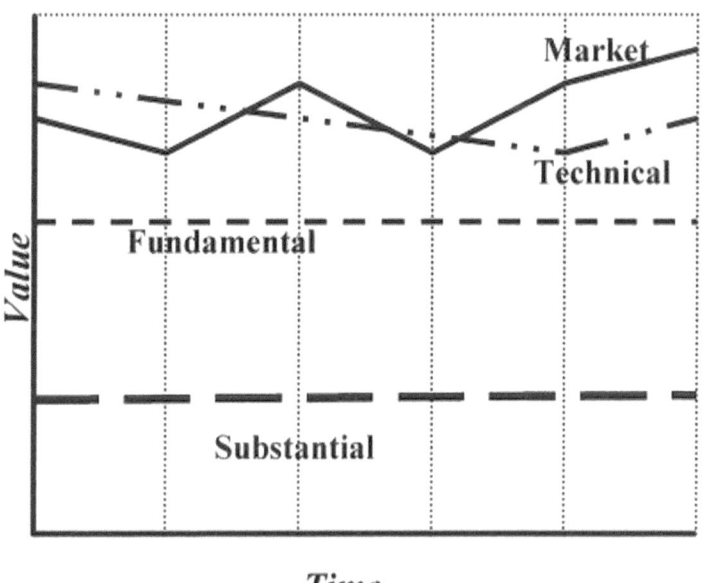

5.3.2 - Future Value

In government markets, returns on investment go along with "government will". That is out of the traditionally known economic concepts. But If we know the "government polices" we also know authorities will try to implement them in their "government market" as time goes by. But conditions present in the bigger democratic market work as a **limitation** against the realization of autocratic controllers will.

The class equation that represents a future value in an influenced mixed market stays like this:

$$P_{Future} = P_{Actual} + G. \text{Will}_{Government} - M. \text{Will}_{Market}$$

Where: P_{Future} is the future price we want to know; P_{Actual} is the actual price that is a reference; **G** is the value introduced by the imponderable factor that represents the objective factor of the will of government; $\text{Will}_{Government}$ is the interference of government in the government market (active=1; inactive=0); **M** is the value introduced by the imponderable factor that represents the objective factor of the will of the market; Will_{Market} is the interference of market participants in the democratic market (active=1; inactive=0);

5.3.3 - Mixed influenced mode market spectrum

The following equations define influence power for the autocratic controllers; and participants; mixed influenced market.

Autocratic Influence = $G. \text{Will}_{Government} / (G+M)$
Democratic Influence = $M. \text{Will}_{Market} / (G+M)$

Influence Spectrum – is a space or "interval composed of aspects and values, in a rule system to where actions of controllers may take market value.

If democratic market is predominant then the autocratic influence on it is small and autocratic controllers need to submit their will to its movements.

Because of this characteristic, influence spectrum is always in the vicinity of current prices. The figure 16 below illustrates this thought;

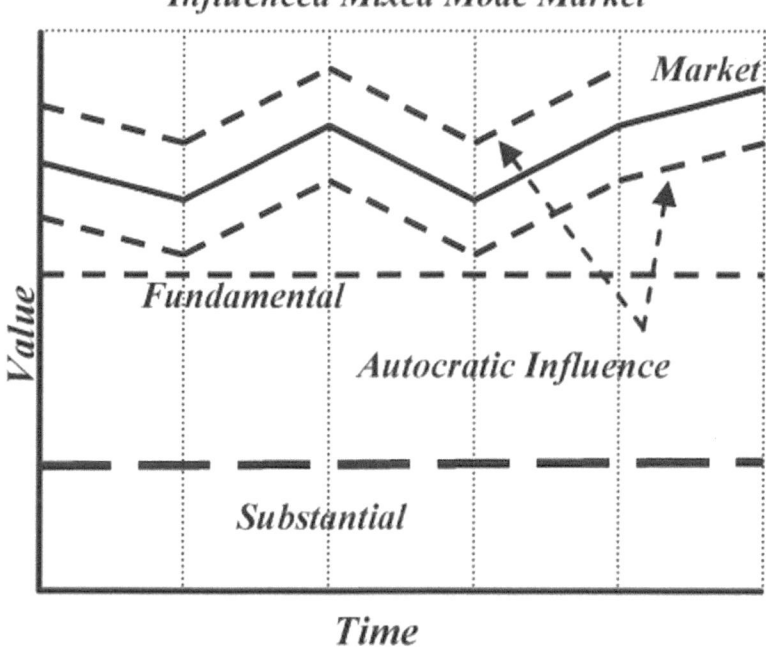

Notice that G may assume any signal depending on the will that introduces it and market conditions. If a government wishes to heighten his company's stock price in the market, then G may assume a different value according to market conditions as a whole.

In a democratic market that is in a high movement; government may simply watch closely such high and do nothing, or he may apply certain amount of recourses to better fulfill his polices.

In a democratic market that is in a downward movement; government will need to put a much bigger amount of recourses to position his influenced prices above market prices.

5.3.4 Political Model

Knowing the controllers polices, the class equation for future value, and the influence spectrum, it is possible for us to establish technical limits for operations in this type of market.

Notice that if government is going out, someone has to mobilize resources to get in his profitable positions. And this money must come from somewhere else them government itself. But such a movement may well be founded by investors from abroad. So there are a range of possibilities that must be addressed in a case by case study.

Remember that autocratic markets are "case sensitive"; each case constitutes a different case. In the medium range of time, destructive objectives may be reached by any strategy. While constructive objectives, require a specific set of strategies, mainly not aggressive. In these mixed influenced mode markets, all goes as if agreements were established at every moment between government and market participants.

Because of this, we shall never use general rules for autocratic market as are being used for democratic markets.

5.4- Operations on influenced mixed mode market

Buy and Sell

When we buy a "stock title" in the "stock market" we attach a certain amount of our resources to that title. And all goes independently of the fact whether we may be in a democratic market or in a government market. Therefore when we use class equation to interpret reality the **differences appear**.

Government decides what he wishes to do with relation to his market. Which one is operated by public employees that being so, conceptually do not get rich with their successes.

That means anything may be their objective. By other side government markets move in phases, rather than in movements as democratic markets do.

Because of all this there is no other way for dealing with government markets, then to find about **government polices** and base our decisions on them. That may be expressed in class equations as follows:

"Expanding profits police" = "prices go up"

"Decision" = "Buy"

Or in the other direction:

"Decreasing profits police" = "prices go down"
"Decision" = "Sell"

Notice that government policies and decisions of participants constitute separate and interactive waves.

Being that the wave "police=Consequence" is totally formed in the mental environment of participants.

And the wave "decision=action" is formed part in the mental environment and other part in the auxiliar space showing information about that stock market. One wave interacts with the other changing its values.

Watching market equilibrium price behavior, we might have some clues about the autocratic controller's polices. And we could make a prevision of future value based on them. But controllers have the faculty to change them at any moment without any prior notice. That would turn our prevision on a bet. Only autocratic market controllers themselves know the exact reasons for their decisions. Therefore we should also look out of the market for answers.

5.5 - Track record of influenced mixed mode market

When we have a government market that operates inside a much bigger democratic market, the democratic mode logical patters are affected by the phases of the government market.

This combination will tend to democratic logic or to autocratic polices in accordance to the extension of government presence on the market as a whole.

If, government presence on it, is small, than democratic logic will prevail. But if it is significant, then political principles may prevail from time to time. We may say that:

"The shortest way between two track points in a preponderantly democratic market with government market inside it is a twisty, cyclical and unforeseen curve"

06 Manipulated Mixed Mode Market

Let us consider now in this chapter, the manipulated mixed mode market.

As a classic example of this type of market, also we have the government stock market but this time it is bigger than a democratic market where it is immersed.

All goes as in influenced markets with some important differences; among then the ones considered below.

1 – Future value on manipulated mix mode market

The class equation that represents a future value in a manipulated mixed market is this:

$$P_{Future} = P_{Actual} + G.\,Will_{Government} - M.\,Will_{Market}$$

So there is no change with relation to the influenced mix mode.

Manipulation Spectrum

Autocratic manipulation spectrum may be expressed as follows.

Autocratic Manipulation = G. Will $_{Government}$ / (G+M)
Democratic Influence = M. Will $_{Market}$ / (G+M)

All goes as in the influenced mixed mode markets but in this case the autocratic influence over the market as a whole is much bigger at the point where autocratic controllers may substitute its natural track by another one that they wish. The value of manipulation spectrum determines until what point controller may alter the natural track of the market. The figure 17 below explains this thought.

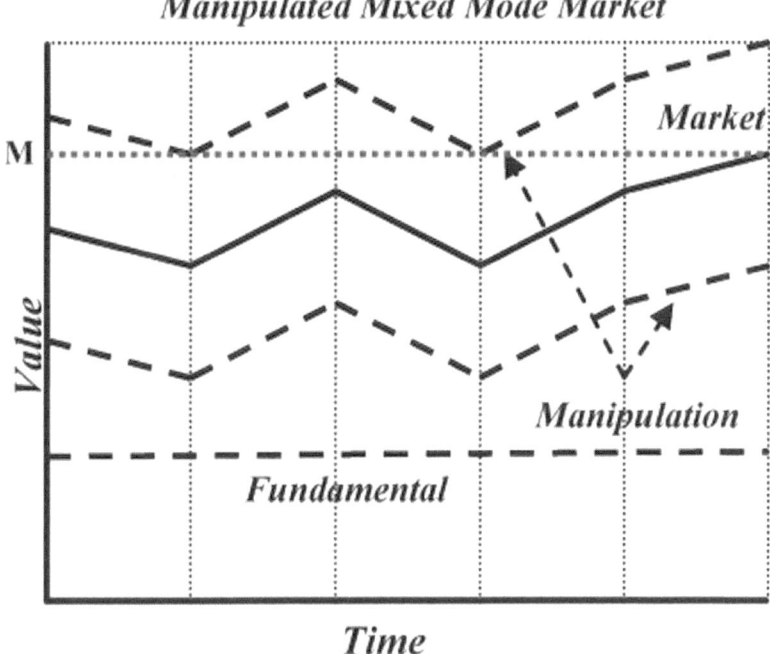

Notice that in this case, if he wishes, the autocratic controller may keep the prices of the market fixed at value "M" (dotted line). Also he may use his strong influence to heighten his position in the market. In the limit the government may establish a state corner in the market.

State corner - is a situation where government has informally taken over the majority or even all activities, stocks, assets, or investments in a particular segment, sector, industry or even market using only his characteristics difference as a differential. Among them his exclusive state power, his centralized command and his contextual activities.

In a situation of state corner government may have prices fixed promoting gains or losses to clients.

2 – Track record of markets in manipulated mix mode

The tracks of manipulated markets are strongly influenced by the will of their autocratic controllers. By this reason we may say that:

"The shortest way between two track points in a democratic market where the presence of a government market is preponderant, is a twisty, cyclical, and sometimes interrupted curve"

CHAPTER 9

CONTROLLED MIXED MODE MARKET

Controlled Mixed Mode Markets are formed mostly by several autocratic mode markets.

Due to absence of fixed references for these markets, and multiplicity of participants classes, and multiplicity of objectives classes, and other differences, controlled mixed markets may materialize in countless forms, each one with its respective "abstract class object" that are different from all the others. That means each controlled mixed market that we find in reality is unique; consequently has basic principles that are different from all other systems.

01 Types of Market Control

A control may present itself in classes, values, and/or tracks of a market. Including it may appear on the main system control; on the primary or secondary market; on the offer or demand or both; on technical values, on fundamental values; or even on various aspects at the same time.

02 Stock Market

A classical case of controlled mixed mode market is a government stock market that operates alongside other autocratic markets formed by consequent agents. Let us analyze this case.

2.1 – Analysis Class (Controlled Mixed Mode)

2.1.1 - Separation of government market

Markets we find in reality are generally classified by "conceptual labels" – normally they are nick- named "free and democratic". Nothing more are told about them.

But in order to understand how objectively they operate, we need to do a class analysis, using all data that we may be able to get about them.

The first step is to separate government market from the rest of the market, because these markets follow different rules and operate in autocratic mode.

To do this we need to sort market companies by value – for instance capitalization value. After this we form an index with the most representative ones. This index will represent the whole market in our analyses about company data. The amount of companies in the index is a function of the concentration of value present in the market place.

For instance: ICap30 – Index of capitalization with the 30 biggest companies in capitalization.

Then we may analyze the rules of companies in the index and find their effective voting control. Than we separate them by type of formation, and with this information we may calculate a government presence index. The bigger this index the greater is the possibility of government control over this market.

2.1.2 - Rank of Control for type Democratic Market

The next step is to rank all classes under class (democratic type market), that is being analyzed, in order to find if it operates in democratic or autocratic mode.

A democratic market in any part of the world has only one classical control ranking that is as follows:

0- Class (Stock Holders)
1- Class (Democratic Companies)
2- Class (Democratic Stock Market)

We need to know if the democratic market we are analyzing constitutes a "Real Class Object" of this class.

For this, we may check in the conceptual dimension – "democratic order" embedded on the legal base – if it concedes to the stock holders the control of these companies. And in the day to day dimension if that command is being materialized.

But in our example let us suppose that a legal base defines the rights of stock holders as follows:

"Companies may issue half its stocks without voting rights. And half plus one electors with voting rights may decide everything about the company"

That means company control is fixed in the hands of a certain group of stock holders that accumulate only 25% of company's capital. So there is an autocratic controller in all these democratic companies; that consequently operate in autocratic mode.

With these data we already may say that we are dealing with a controlled market, once government and market operate in autocratic mode.

2.1.3 - Offer and Demand Subclasses

Still we need to continue our research to find more about the depth of the controlling process. We know it may occur in all subclasses of that market.

Let us turn our attention to offer and demand.

Watching the "abstract class object" expressed partially in its results report we find that:

Percent participation in the offer and demand:

    1- Class (Foreign Investors) (33%)
    2- Class (Institutional Investors) (33%)
    3- Class (Individual Participants) (30%)
    4- Class (Other Participants) (4%)

We need to analyze each of these classes to look for autocratic control.

Class (Foreign Investors)

Again, analyzing the legal base in search of the democratic order, referring to this point, we discover that foreigners are allowed to operate only through stock funds. That let them vulnerable to government direct order. But it does not mean they are controlled; it means they compete in an organized fashion. We call **Client** to those that compete in a mixed controlled market.

Class (Institutional Investors)

In case of institutions let us suppose we found that indeed they are pension funds of government companies' employees. Government officials may be in their board of directors, they may have majority voting power, and thus they may be heavy influencer on, or even bear responsibility for all those institutions actions.

All this means government may control institutional offer and demand in that market. Which one in its turn, constitutes 33% of offer and demand processes as a whole.

Class (Personal Investors)

Considering that this stock market is located within a government system where more than 92% of people are **supported** by government officials, we may say that few people can really afford to invest money or even speculate in this stock market. So, it is not possible to explain where this high percentage of individual investors comes from. We simply cannot say that with the data we are considering. Because of this we shall consider them also as Clients.

Class (Balance Statements)

Finally analyzing balance sheet statements of democratic market companies, we find that the great majority of them have debt with government in their balance sheets. They have received loans, incentives and other entitlements from government officials. Also government owns some stocks in most of them. That lets them vulnerable to government influence.

Conclusion

Considering that government controls one third of offer and demand, controls government companies, and may influence great part of democratic market; we may conclude that in this case, government control over this whole market wave is very clear.

2.1.4 - Rank of Controlled Mixed Market

Rank for this market class is like this:

    0- Class (Government)

    1- Subclass (Government Market Stocks)
    1- Subclass (Democratic Market Controllers)
    1- Subclass (Democratic Market Stocks)
    1- Subclass (Institutional Investors)

    2- Subclass (Stock Market)

    3- Subclass (Foreign Investors)
    3- Subclass (Personal Investors)

Notice that above Subclass (Stock Market), we find all subclasses of the government and above all that, we find Class (Government). And as subclass of Class (Stock Market), we find **Clients** foreign and personal investors. That is, the **controllers** are above the market and the clients are under the stock market class.

2.2 – Behavior and future value in controlled mixed mode

In a Controlled mixed market we find various autocratic markets that are preponderant over democratic ones if there are any. As we know autocratic markets operate according to polices that are dictated by their controllers, they have different basic principles and objectives, and always they are trying to control more people by their commands.

Thus we have various markets with different characteristics and objectives, each one intending to impose its stile and reach its own objectives, over all other whole market participants.

This phenomenon conveys to controlled mixed markets a characteristic track, that identify them, in a way that is different from any single autocratic or democratic market that may form the whole market.

We may segment and classify these characteristic tracks in three periods as follows:

Alignment
Competition
Dispute

2.2.1 - Alignment Period

A controlled mixed market is in an **alignment** period, when there is an autocratic controller that controls great part or even the whole markets destine.

This alignment is obtained through agreements of the strong among their diverse autocratic controllers; where it is agreed upon interests, means and objectives, to be pursued, used and reached by all market as a whole.

Because of these agreements an aligned controlled mixed market assumes characteristics of an autocratic system that operates alone or with no significantly influent markets.

We call **master controller** or market controller to the class that controls the wave of controllers of an aligned controlled mixed market.

We call controllers to the participants that are aligned with the market controller of an aligned controlled mixed market through agreement of strong contracts.

We call **clients** to those that compete in a mixed controlled market.

Clients in an aligned controlled market exert so little influence that they do not appear in the market class equation for this period. It is up for market controller to determine the track record for this type of market in alignment period, taking into consideration the agreement of strong contract. Class equation for this period is as follows:

$$P_{Future} = P_{Actual} + T \cdot Will_{Controller}$$

Where: P_{Future} is the future price we want to know; P_{Actual} is the actual price that is a reference for future value; T is an objective value introduced by the imponderable will; $Will_{Controller}$ is the imponderable factor that affects the market (active =1; inactive = 0).

Due to the absence of competition or opposition, an aligned Controlled market may reach more efficiently their controller's objectives.

Government Market controllers may lead these aligned markets to reach record values in price and volume; including if they coordinate their market activities with selective, and quality differentiation processes on the democratic environment.

These processes move prices in some aspects in the same market sense - that is "up". And move prices, in all other, infinite aspects in opposite sense – that is; "down".

For instance, in an aligned mixed stock market; stock prices and company profits soar to records each time higher, while at the same time, work price plunge to record lows, and dependency climbs to record highs. **Dependency** is government help to pay bills or investments of people.

In such case it is clear there is a coordination of government mercantilism with differentiation and disqualification of democratic environment. For instance a country makes an agreement to sell minerals through a controlled stock market company to another country, where negative differentiation is very high on its prices. And in return allow that country to sell all it wishes at devaluated prices, to all nom stock market participants.

As a consequent result, stock market prices go much higher and nom stock market prices go down taking out of business whole segments of that economy.

2.2.2 - Competition Period

A Controlled mixed market is in a **competition** period, when there is an autocratic controller which tries to control the whole markets destine, but faces significant competition from another part of the market that also wants to control it.

Two classes are important in the class equation that represents a competition period mixed market; Controllers and Clients. And the class equation goes like this:

$$P_{Future} = P_{Actual} + T.\,Will_{Controller} - C.\,Will_{Clients}$$

Where: C is a value introduced into the equation by the will of clients. Will $_{Clients}$ is an imponderable factor (Active = 1; Inactive = 0) that represents the will of Clients.

The stronger controllers in a competition mixed market mode want to conquer and subdue clients. But clients in return impose significant limits against their actions in the market.

Notice that controllers can be inactive for some time (imponderable factor = 0). In this case market will simply attend the will of clients. That means, simply watching a stock section, may not be enough to classify a market in this period. We need to do a class analyses for this purpose.

And the track this market goes on follows the result from the interaction among those two participant classes.

For instance, values may strongly oscillate around medium values above or under natural market value.

When clients are subclass of international market participants' classes, they may draw down or up the prices of competition market according to fluctuations in their origin international market classes.

The movement intensity against the will of controllers shall depend on their own wiliness to pay the costs associated to contain such move.

Controllers may manage their interference in the market in order to obtain their objectives by lowering costs of intervention.

For instance when market is excessively in a seller mood, against their will they may let prices float freely, and only after that, they may try to restore things to where they wish them to be.

2.2.3 - Dispute Period

Eventually there may be a dispute over control of the Controlled mixed market. This is the **Dispute** Period.

Notice that by the natural order of things we need to mobilize much more value to create something in value, than to destroy this same thing in value.

For instance, think of the resources we need to create an apartment building and after this think what we do need to destroy it. That is, fewer resources are necessary to destroy things than to build them.

This natural principle is worth for everything in our life, including the markets.

Thus the simple destruction of adversary value is the main tactics used in a dispute by the various autocrat controllers that want to control the whole market. To do this, they may fist devalue themselves putting their adversaries in a difficult situation by interaction. And do whatever is needed to accomplish their aims.

The one who subdues the other wins the control of the whole Controlled market system.

This phenomenon in its maximum expression is indeed what is behind the urban war that occurs in many deficient systems among various armed groups, exactly fighting for supremacy against all others, and the consequent control of the deficient system.

In the Controlled mixed market the effect of that phenomenon is a consistent and significant value loss. So big that may seem illogical by some observers, but in deed represent the damages done one another by the participants in the dispute.

By the other side, notice that, a whole democratic environment constitutes a mixed market, where there are many autocratic systems, competing with each other.

And being so, a whole stock market also may enter in a dispute with the democratic environment outside it.

Such a dispute may occur for instance because of an imminent, or recently occurred, political philosophy change.

Many imponderable factors may become active in a dispute deepening yet more the value loss in such market place. For instance, foreign investors may simply go home reacting to imminent or recently occurred order that threatens to jeopardize foreign investments.

Yet by another side, notice that even democratic market operating in democratic mode, may suddenly enter in dispute with the rest of the democratic environment due to some aggression that threatens its participants as a whole.

For this reason, in dispute periods the Controlled mixed markets may present strong depression in its prices. The class equation that expresses the future value in these markets goes as follows.

$$P_{Future} = P_{Actual} + T \cdot Will_{Controller} - U \cdot Will_{Autocrats} - C \cdot Will_{Clients}$$

Where: P_{Future} is the future price we want to know; P_{Actual} is the actual price that is a reference; T is an objective value introduced by the imponderable will of wave controllers; U is an objective value introduced by the imponderable will of other autocrats; C is a value introduced into the equation by the imponderable will of **clients**; $Will_{Controller}$ imponderable will of controllers (active =1; Inactive = 0); $Will_{Autocrats}$ imponderable will of other autocrats (active =1; Inactive = 0); $Will_{Clients}$ imponderable will of **clients** (Active = 1; Inactive = 0).

2.2.4 - Controlled Market Mode Spectrum

The following class equations define intervention power of controllers of Controlled mixed mode markets:

Aligned Controlled:
Controller Intervention Power = $T \cdot Will_{Controller}$

Competing Controlled:

Controller Intervention Power = **T. Will** $_{Controller}$ / (T+C)

Disputed Controlled:

Controller Intervention Power = **T. Will** $_{Controller}$ / (T+ U+C)
Autocratic Intervention Power = **U. Will** $_{Autocrats}$ / (T+ U+C)

Spectrum of a market is a time interval in the proper rule environment where market track may occur.

In a Controlled market the spectrum shows the possible periods it may be. The following figure 18 illustrates such a spectrum:

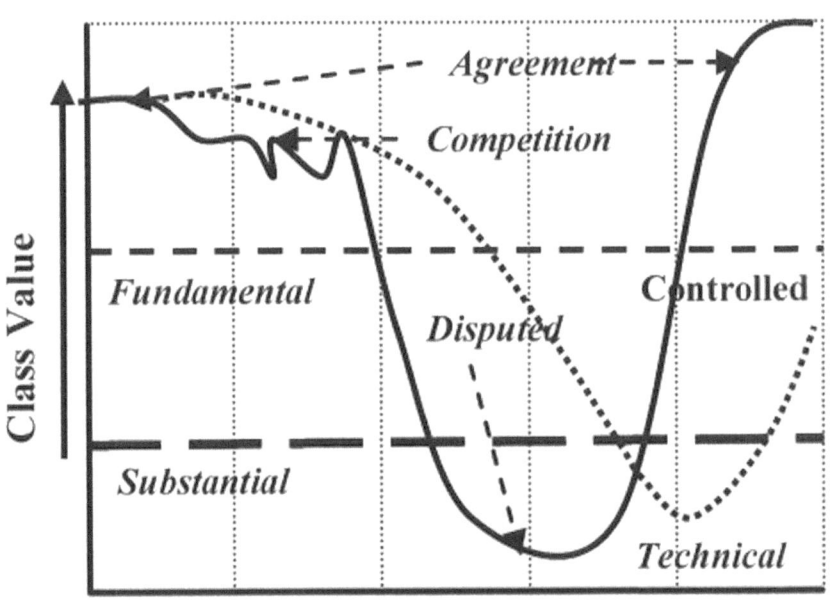

This illustration calls our attention to the following points:

1. An aligned Controlled market may present itself in higher than expected prices – much higher than fundamental prices- that seems to be staying forever.

2. A competition market may present itself by strong and aimless price oscillation. This is a result of the struggle the controller faces to sell his prices to clients that want better conditions. At the end of competition period market prices may plunge very firmly.

3. A disputed market may present itself with prices stable but so low as fundamental or even substantial prices. And they may remain in this situation until a new agreement of the strong can be formed in the market environment.

4. When finally, a new agreement of the strong is reestablished market rallies up for alignment situation again.

5. The passing from a dispute period to an alignment period distribute profits for all those who are positioned in the long side of these markets. That means even persons not acquainted with any market at all become excellent investors. They are tide-waiters that simply appear to profit from the opportunity.

6. An alignment period that goes into competition period and into dispute period may distribute imposed losses to everybody positioned in the long side of the market.

7. A long range investor will need patience to see the strong fluctuation of his portfolio among disputes and alignment, which individually may endure long periods of time.

8. But stocks that guarantee control may be separated and transacted by buyer and seller off the counter, independently of

market price of the stocks with no control rights. Thus controller may have some immunity with relation to market periods. But they are not immune with respect to their day to day operations.

We are not speaking of phases here because any of these periods may stay indefinitely. A market may remain in dispute, competition or alignment even forever. It is very important to understand the history of its context to know the usage of the place as a whole and possible change in market historic patter.

We should always be aware that will of people - that move things in reality - is a mental environment phenomenon.

2.3 – Operations – Controlled Mixed Mode Markets

Buy and Sell

We must be aware of the periods of these markets as a basic guide line for our operations. Inside these periods of the market as a whole, we may find the various phases of its various individual autocratic markets being developed as well. Each one according to individual polices commanded by their controllers. That is, autocratic parts of the market individually may be gowing or contracting, and democratic part of the market may be in upward movement or in downward movement. All this inside the same period be it what it may be.

A period of tough **dispute** with strong depression in prices may present itself as an excellent opportunity to amass big gains, for those who wish to enter these markets and can wait their **alignment** period to come. Some disputes may be quickly solved; others may even not be solved at all. But Controlled markets derive from stable rule conditions that cannot be easily changed. Because of that, their participants need to search an alignment in order to maximize their return.

In the opposite side of the spectrum, a market that is in alignment and starts a period of competition may be the right moment to sell and wait till dispute comes in, to buy again.

Track

Considering all that was showed in this chapter we may say that: "The shortest way between two track points in a Controlled mixed market is a twisty, cyclical, periodical, and sometimes interrupted, or unachievable, curve".

CHAPTER 10

EXISTENTIAL ENVIRONMENT

In this chapter we will show you the **existential environment** according to the objective theory.

01 Existential Environment

Existential environment is a class that forms all that exists in reality and in unreality.

Reality environment is composed of nature, society and the considered proper rule environment.

Unreality environment is composed of mental and sovereign environments.

All these environments are indeed integrated with each other in real life – that is, they constitute a whole - but for the Objective Theory they are considered to be separated and all relations between them are taken into account, each one separately - it is a segmented way to observe reality.

This separation allows us to observe many phenomena otherwise not seen. It is just like one pair of glasses that help us to observe things.

EXISTENTIAL ENVIRONMENT

02 Environment Symbols and Representation

There are symbols for each one of these environments as follows in figure 19 according to their class rank:

Head without face — Sovereign Environment	
Man with arms stretched — Mental Environment	
Atom — Nature Environment	
Chain — Social Environment	
Equilibrium Balance — Proper Rule Environment	

All other environments interact with the rule system forcibly changing its values. Because of this, when relating a rule system environment to another environment, we may face many dilemmas; for instance; "what will be the social agent's decision?" According to the objective theory, all these dilemmas are solved by the application of one or a group of **natural principles**.

Natural Principles are basic ideas that exist in nature, upon which all rules in all areas of life are organized. Together they constitute the **natural order of things,** and they appear in all study areas in different forms. When we create a new area of study we may simply import them from other study areas and give the appropriate form to function in the new study area.

Within the Objective Theory Study Areas, natural principles and the natural order of things assume objective forms and solve all, the otherwise unsolvable, dilemmas. The following design in figure 20 represents in a graphic form, all the existential environments, and their imponderable interference in the considered rule system:

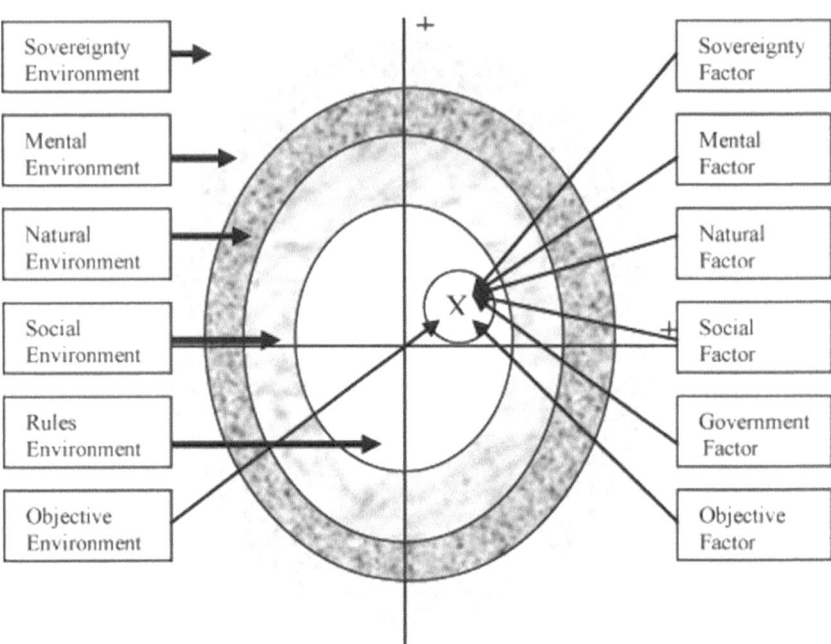

In the right side of the figure, we have the five existential environments, plus the in reality, consequently on any auxiliar objective space when it is considered the reference environment. "X" represents an objective value that is influenced by the objective factors produced by the 5 existential environments. In the left side we have the 5 imponderable factors that introduce the respective objective factors that affect the value of "X".

03 Environmental Interactions

The **natural order of things** allows us to describe some characteristics of the environmental interactions with rule systems as follows in this section. The Objective Theory segments the environment Class (Existence) in 5 subclasses, and establishes its ranks according to the **natural order of things**, as follows:

0- Class (Existence Environment)
1- Subclass (Sovereign Environment)
2- Subclass (Mental Environment)
3- Subclass (Nature environment)
4- Subclass (Society environment)
5- Subclass (Rule environment)

We call **unreality** environment to the **sovereign** and **mental** environments altogether. We call **reality** environment to **rule**, **society** and **nature** environment altogether. Thus we may also express the class rank of existence environment wave as follows:

0- Class (Existence Environment)
1- Subclass (Unreality)
3- Subclass (Reality)

Let us consider each one of these subclasses isolated from the others.

04 Unreality Environments

Unreality environments do not need resource mobilization for creating and altering their phenomena. They constitute classes and abstract objects. As we said it is formed by **sovereign** and **mental** environments.

1 – Subclass (Sovereign Environment)

The sovereignty Environment has absolute power over all other environments. It is integrated by all sovereignty power there may exist in all existential being, altogether or individually.

The sovereignty environment is in charge of the decision-making production.

Through decision making, it manages all existence; and through its interference all things comes to exist, or are extinct. This means **sovereignty** environment attributions can not be executed by any other inferior environment.

Also, it is up to the sovereignty environment certain functions that produce objects that come to exist in our day to day life, but we have no natural explanation for them; such as miracles, luck, destine and karmas.

Through miracles some natural rules are not fulfilled when some good thing is formed; through luck someone is favored by facts and an opportunity appears; and through destine someone achieves a surprising objective.

2 – Subclass (Mental Environment)

The mental environment has power over all reality environments. And, submits itself to the sovereign environment. It is integrated by all thinking power that may exist in all existential beings, altogether or individually.

If you watch reality, as some researchers have done before us, certainly you will find fixed patters for creation, extinction, formation and development of all things in life.

In other words, all that exists are created, or formed, and develop themselves in accordance with patterns that may be identified and classified. We call these patters **classes**.

These classes occur in all the environments subject to the sovereignty environment. Including, mental environment itself. Thou, all things **do exist** in reality and in thoughts in accordance to some patterns - or **Classes**.

The mental environment is in charge of identifying these classes.

It processes all issues related to known classes, and sends for sovereignty decision, the ones referring to not known classes. This means, many processes involving **value destruction** may be managed only through mental environment, following previous simple known **thought patters**. This readiness may in some extent end up causing some imposed losses to many people. For instance, we immediately thought one way about something and it was different.

04 Reality Environments

Nature environment along with society, and rule environments constitute reality. The **realty** environments have in common the fact that they need **mobilization** of resources to **produce things**.

4.1 – Subclass (Nature environment)

Natural aspects and natural agents influence in a determined way the rule system environment. In reality nobody is able to deceive natural rules. Because of this **supremacy order**, any proper rule system order which violates natural principles, are simply **useless, and not operant**.

Natural order supersedes any society and proper rule order. We cannot change natural principles by proper rule system rules. But some natural principles may form events only in accordance to some social or proper rule agent action or inaction. For example; one agent's natural sex is not avoidable, but the procreation occurs only if he or she, does some specific things. Notice that in this book we do not discuss things such as faith, miracles, lucky, destiny etc.…

4.2 – Subclass (Society environment)

Social aspects and agents influence the rule system environment in an imponderable way. Since it is a subjective environment something in one society may cause a huge interference in its government rule system, but the same thing in other society may cause opposite effect or no effect at all.

The social effect over any rule system may be determined only by the use of class equation. The natural order of things determines the supremacy of social conventions over the democratic order. That means you are not able to change social behavior by a rule order.

In spite of this, that is precisely what some set of rules try to do in many deficient or inefficient systems that we find in reality. They simple try to change social conventions by means of government order.

That is precisely why many undesired phenomena occur in deficient or inefficient systems with increased frequency and intensity. By the other side, a simple social convention (good or bad) may end up inside the rule system set of rules generating a range of democratic commands that impose losses or concede gains to some or even all system participants.

4.3 – Subclass (Rule environment)

4.3.1 – Basic Parts

All **rule** system is compounded of a **set of rules**, an **actuating** environment, and a **consequent** environment. Every time someone creates a single or a set of rules, to be followed by someone, than a **rule system** has been created or modified if already existed – as shown in figure 1.

The set of rules is a space. The **actuating** and **consequent** environments are environments. Any rule system is formed by one space and two environments. They are called **basic parts** of the rule system, because where there is one of them, also there has to be the other two. Because of this characteristic we may call a system simply referring to one of its **basic parts**.

We call **Rule** environment to the set formed by the actuating environment plus consequent environment.

It is very important to understand that a **rule system** is physically formed only by **people** that obey a particular **set of rules**. We call each of these people **participants**, or **agents**. A Rule System is simply a group of people that agree or are forced to fulfill a particular set of rules.

4.3.2 – Agents

The **consequent environment** is formed by **consequent agents** - who obey orders enforced by actuating agents.

The **actuating environment** is formed by **actuating agents** – who enforce orders onto the consequent agents.

Notice that any **actuating agent** is a **consequent agent** in all aspects where he is not actuating.

One person becomes a rule consequent agent when fulfills the admittance specifications and is admitted into the system. One person becomes actuating Agent when is approved into these functions by superior classes of actuating agents.

4.3.3 – Attributes

Thus, in a rule system you do not have enterprises, cars, houses, dogs, children, son, family, and mountain, for instance.

All social and natural values constitute attributes – or coordinates belonging to agents.

Example, a car is an attribute of the participant who socially owns it; a son is an attribute of the participant who naturally and socially has it.

We call democratic or rule attributes to those associated to an agent through the set of rule.

For instance, the balance someone has in an official or government bank is a democratic attribute. A resource someone has in an informal business is not a democratic attribute because there is no law regulating it.

But in this case, it is an attribute in the informal rule system to which the owner belongs.

4.3.4 – Classes of democratic systems

These rule systems may be classified according to their nature in three classes:

Government System class - are the ones that conceptually pursue well being of all participants, and where **actuating agents,** do have **exclusive state power.**

Exclusive state power is the power to force people to do, or not to do things according to the set of rules. Government systems basic parts may be also called; **Democratic Thinking, State** and **Democracy** in place of set of rules, actuating environment and consequent environment.

Democracy is a set of people who obey orders enforced by State.

State is a set of people who enforce order onto democracy.

Official System classes – are those formed in the consequent environment, by agents that do not have exclusive state power. They resort to government systems to enforce their rights, and are influenced and regulated by them.

Informal system classes – are those that we create in our everyday life. They require no official regulation, nor any fixed standard for functioning, and are influenced by all others.

4.3.5 – Reference

Rule systems must be considered to be a reference. All that does not belong to a referenced rule system belongs to society and nature relative to that system. So, if we consider a rule system corresponding socially to a corporation, then all else, is its society including the government rule system itself inside which, that considered system exists.

We call **Objective Environment** to the system that is being considered **consequent dimension**.

4.3.6 – Dimensions

According to Objective Theory, dimensions are classes of abstract spaces where phenomena may occur on the proper rule system. All actions and events in proper rule systems forms ideas in specific dimensions. There are four dimensions where these ideas may happen:

Conceptual – where thoughts occur

Actuating – where enforcement actions occur

Consequent – where consequent actions occur, and consequent results appear

Day to Day – where consequent results are integrated in reality or unreality.

One event in the conceptual dimension may pass on to actuating dimension, then pass on to the consequent dimension, and end up on day to day dimension. Where it interacts with all other aspects of existence and becomes a part of it.

Through dimensions the whole proper rule system is directly connected to reality.

Social Idea →(Conceptual →Actuating →Consequent →Day to Day)

Social ideas are any concepts we may see in any area – that may be studied by various specialists, or even passed down through generations, by fashion, curiosity etc....

Society is the outside side of any referenced democratic system – simply that!

In other words, just to clarify this idea, society is the whole world **except the referred proper rule system in question**. Do not worry, we'll delve deeper into that in the next book!

All proper Rule System phenomena, have an objective nature.

Because of this feature, objectivation is a logical process to make objective expression out of any idea that goes into the system. After that participants objectively produce a new rule to be inserted in the set of rules. If objectivation is not possible, the idea is simply dismissed.

The set of rules is a very well-defined space that contains the principles and other rules for one system. As well as actuating environment (defined by statutes), and consequent environment (defined by the official data about all participants). Each of these parts of the system has its own dimension where things are formed (in reality and in unreality realm - dimension). There are three parts in the proper rule system but four dimensions where phenomena may occur; why is that? Because the Day to Day dimension occurs in real life, where consequent results are delivered to the world. Let's say it is the integration of consequent results with all other aspects of existence. For example:

We have a Factory of product K

Set of rules; will establish how it shall work - That is Conceptual Dimension

Operators use machines and methods in order to make K – That is Actuating Dimension.

Consequent agents; inspect products coming from the machines and may stock them in some prepared place – That is Consequent Dimension.

Product K then is sold to buyers and integrate reality – That is Day to Day Dimension.

A democratic system of government may be established inside any so-called form of statehood leadership, because it relates only to its participants. That means it can exist under one; King, Sultan, Dictator or President with statesmanship rule, etc. That means NATION is a social concept, and proper rule system is an operating process. We can have a head of any nation and its democratic operating system working very well; hearing and heeding subject opinions consequently reducing losses for that nation as a whole.

05 Democratic Order

The Perfect Democratic System is indeed an abstract representation of the best possible system construed by, governed by, and with the purpose of serving its participants, considered all and every one equal. (this is exactly what some religious believe is how our Mighty God created human beings; equal, and in his resemblance).

Yet, in existence there is no one equal to another. So, the Perfect Democratic System, can not materialize in reality. It exists only in the Conceptual Dimension. It is an objective to be pursued by those wishing a better life.

The democratic order (in the conceptual dimension) conceptually, is formed from, but is not part of, the set of rules of a democratic system. The set of rules is supposed to be a registry of orders we want to enforce onto the system; but things simply written, or spoken in any place, do not automatically materialize in reality.

So, Democratic Order is formed out of reality itself and exists in conceptual dimension:

Democratic Order ← Reality

Democratic Order → Reality

Both ways are correct for relations among democratic order and reality

It has infinite aspects with their respective infinite values, and really makes things happen in reality. It is very fluid and needs no resources to change, that is why we need a class study to detect some of its aspects at any given time - it is not written anywhere.

One big challenge we face when solving reality problems is precisely identifying the greatest amount of aspects and values involved in class equations originated from the democratic order (also called "democratic thinking"); but we will always be short in this challenge. The more we get of them, the better off we shall be in accomplishing our goals.

Deficient or Inefficient systems may present a democratic order substantially different from what is written in their set of rules (deficient, or inefficient). More efficient systems tend to have more efficient set of rules- that fits more with reality we witness in reality. Notice that we may call "reality" when referring to "existence". It is just a more understandable form of speech.

06 Classical Registries of Existence Events

A fundamental rule in Lirian Mathematics is that: "An abstract class object only corresponds to a real class object if it has coordinates in all existential environment". This rule may be referred to as "the five-environmental nature of existential values". All that exists have coordinates in each and every one of the five existential environments.

1 – Class equation representation

An existential number– **five- environmental number** - representing anything, be it a person, animal or any other thing, may be represented as a five environmental class wave. As is expressed below:

Existential Value = X
+ G. Imponderable Factors $_{Government}$
+ S. Imponderable Factors $_{Society}$
+ N. Imponderable Factors $_{Nature}$
+ R. Imponderable Factors $_{Rule}$
+ M. Imponderable Factors $_{Mental}$
+ V. Imponderable Factors $_{Sovereign}$

Where X is an objective number and all the others are objective factors introduced by imponderable factors (Active=1; Inactive=0) "describing" resultant of the infinite aspects where that number has coordinates.

2 – Cartesian Representation

Since every one of the infinite aspects of the existence environment are classic independent from all the others. And all subclasses of that environment also contain infinite independent aspects; finally considering the Object Theory five subclasses of the existential environment; Then we can represent any real number with their five-environmental coordinates. The following figure 21 illustrates a representation in coordinate axis of a **five-environmental number**:

Five-environmental number

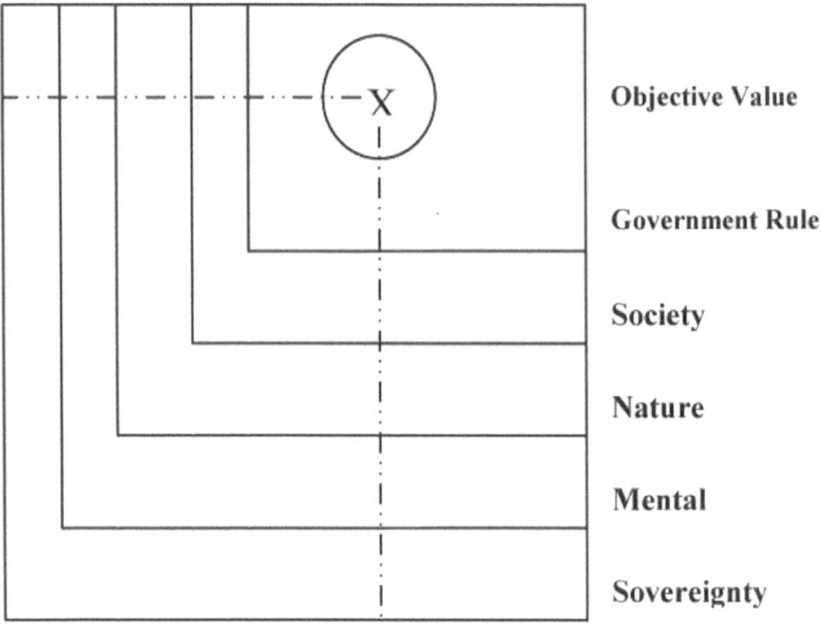

Notice that these environments are shown in this figure in order of importance from the outer most axes (Sovereignty) to the lesser important environment (Objective value).

3 – Classical Representation

Lirian Mathematics allows us to express in **consequent** and **conceptual dimension** all existential values we want to consider. Any "real object" has its **corresponding "abstract class object"** and this in its turn has its **original class**. The following figure 22 illustrates the classical expression of **existential values**.

EXISTENTIAL ENVIRONMENT

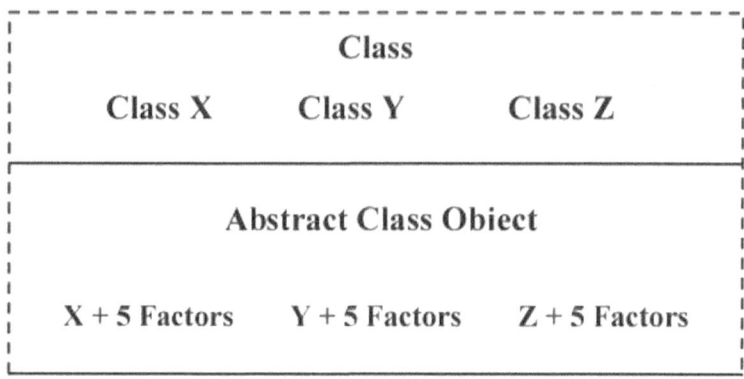

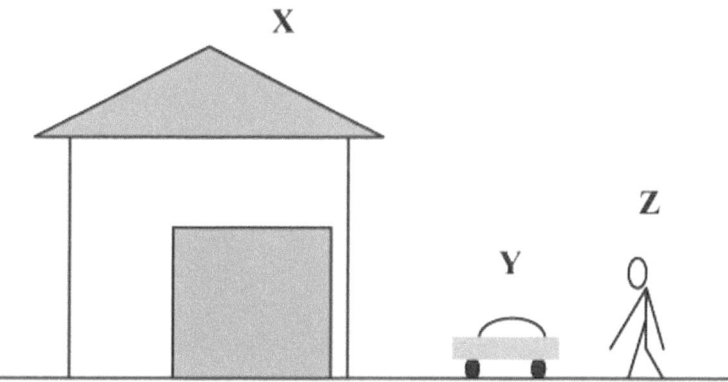

In this figure the word **"Factors"** substitutes the necessary sets of infinite factors and respective objective values in each of the 5 existential environments.

Notice that:

   a - Only some of the infinite existential factors may be effectively expressed in any **objective registry (or auxiliar place; piece of paper, computer archive, etc.)** All the infinite others are, abstractly located in people's mental environment. This is the same phenomena for example, you find in any construction project, any plumb project, any personal report, any automobile user's guide, etc.

b - **Class** and "**abstract class objects**" do exist in the mental environment of people. But their "**objective registry**" and their corresponding "**real objects**" do exist in reality.

c - **Unreal objects** cannot be observed in **reality** because they do not have material expression.

CHAPTER 11

EXISTENTIAL DYNAMICS

In this chapter we shall discuss some concepts about existential evolution; the integrated environment class it forms - that we call Life Environment or Life Experience; and about realization of future class objects.

01 Class (Life Environment)

All of us certainly have heard a lot about past, present and future. But in the Democratic Game and System Objective Theory we need to import these social concepts to the objective democratic environment, and give them objective versions that are unique. Notice that we only study the democratic system and its interactions with other environments; not any other environments themselves.

The objective theory accepts the idea that the **existential environment** "moves in time". That is, it "travels in time". And as it moves, it defines a region in the form of a tube. And this tube constitutes the integrated environment called **Life Environment**. So this environment is a succession of Positions in time of Existential environment one after the other according to the passage of time. Different from the others this is an integrated environment, that's why we also may call it Life Experience.

Class (Life Environment) is formed by three different integrated environment subclasses, which are; **Class (Present), Class (Past)** and **Class (Future).**

Class (Present) - is formed by the actual existential position plus a succession of past existential positions, perceived as similar.

The "abstract class object" as a whole of the Class (Present) is called "project"; and the "real class object" is called "reality". When we refer to parts of the whole there are many names for them, including; "balance sheet", "statement", "session" – for abstract class objects; and "things", "people", "land escape" – for real class objects.

Of course reality changes minute by minute. So, when we have a significant change in things, we say those changed things stayed in the past. **Novelty is the present**.

Class (Past) – this is formed by all that is not more in the present. The abstract class object of the past is collectively called "history", and in particular is called "past events". In order to discover something in the past, we need to redefine each of the existential environments at the time, before we research what we want to find.

Class (Future) – is formed by abstract existential positions that may or may not realize as time goes by. The abstract class objects of the future are "thoughts" and "decisions". Many of these never realize due to competition, mobilization, and interaction phenomena among others. The following figure 23 illustrates these concepts:

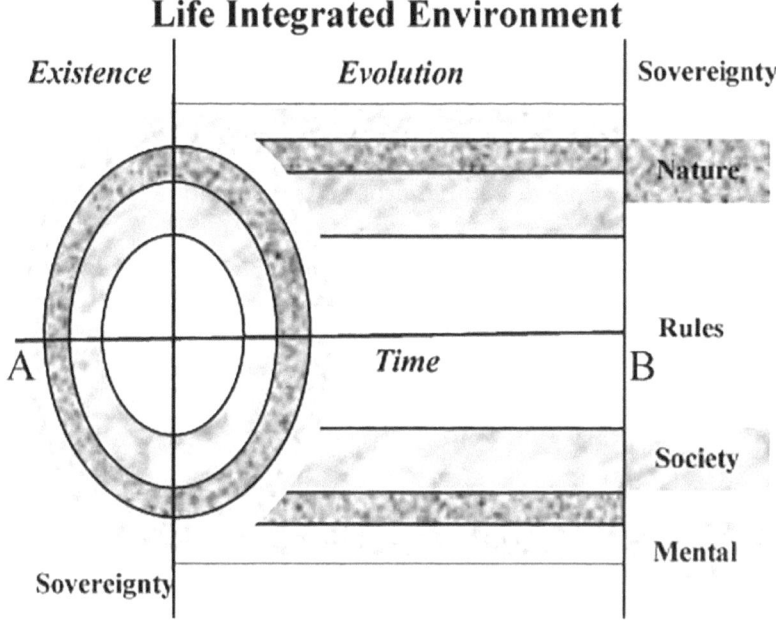

Where; line AB represents time; existence is the actual position or present; and evolution is history.

Time - may be counted from any existential position that we decide to initiate the counting on.

Existential position - is the existential environment considered static in some given moment. It includes **objective consequence** and **imponderable influence**.

Imponderable influence is all that may be pressing the objective consequence, including agent's will, and systemic goals.

02 Objective Existential Dynamics

<u>**Objective Existential Dynamics**</u> - studies dynamics characteristics and evolution of existential environment in time. It is divided into several other sub areas. Here are some important concepts:

2.1 – Real values; a long time

The real environments change as times goes by. Earth, animals, plants assume new positions, some disappear other come to existence, we get older, fatter, and thinner, something gains or losses utility, friendships are created or are ended, and the proper rules gain or lose effect.

Because of this, we cannot tell in the present the profile of future situations in real environments. Even knowing that animals, for instance, present themselves in nature in accordance to known patters, we cannot even affirm that they will continue to exist, as many races have already been extinct. Hence comes, the universal principle of indetermination of real situations in time – or simply the **future indetermination principle**.

Real situations naturally evolve in time in an undetermined way.

2.2 – Unreal values in time

Decision – the sovereignty environment is free from time and space; it decides with sovereignty what may exist in all other environments. But an agent's decision may realize things that are undesired to others. Because of this, agents do compete to decide who will realize what wants.

The sovereign agent's decision will prevail over a dependent agent's decision in any relation.

Natural Agents – transform reality along with human beings. Notice that in natural environment any living or inanimate things constitute an agent and may surge sometimes **"from nowhere"** to realize **"real class objects"**; for instance; storms, hurricanes, bacteria, viruses, chemical elements and materials.

Thought - is free of time and space. However, it changes as time goes by in accordance with decisions taken by the thinker. We think one way in one day, and other way in other day; and this occurs without any relation to time or space. But: We think only in accordance to our own decision to think.

Notice that people, who lived thousands of years before us, were able to express actual thoughts, the same way as many people who live today are certainly able to express thoughts that will prevail in a distant future.

As mental environment presents itself segmented and individually distributed through agents: An agent may think what he wishes even not related to the rule system, and not agreeable to other agents.

Thought limits – as sovereignty environment rules over mental environment, we may, somehow, decide to impose some restrictions on our thoughts. So, we may say that our thoughts are limited only by our own decisions.

2.3 – Class (Thought Filter)

Thought filter – is a limit imposed by us to our thinking capability. For better understanding class (thought filters), let us do a simple analogy with information flux on a television set:

A TV set may transmit all the information that it is able to capture in its region. We do not have domain over this information. Which ones, are technically grouped in TV channels. But we do have the domain over our TV set, to make it transmit to us only one of these channels of information. The one we chose.

That means we **do not receive all** information that may be transmitted by our TV set, but only those we chose to receive.

This same phenomenon happens in the mental environment; we also apply to it the tuning channel concept.

Mental tuning channels or **thought filters** - constitute themselves in thinking **options** – or **classes** - with known characteristics that we may chose to tune in, and think of.

Using a **"thought filter"** we decide what must exist in our mental environment; for instance; positive thinking (what is good), negative thinking (what is bad), illusions (what cannot exist) and so on.

Notice that **censorship** hides from us, something that exists and we cannot think about what we do not know of.

03 Existential Evolution

3.1 – Existential Evolution

Existential Evolution is the effect of time passage on the existential environment.

At any moment existence has evolved from the past to the present, and is going to the future. That is, present moves along with time. But to obtain present as a fixed reference for our calculations, we have to accept the idea that future is the one which comes to the present, and then the present goes to the past. Present is Class ("Existence" in time = 0)

Real values occur in the present. But a person's **thought** may be in the present, as well as advanced in the future, or yet traveling through past facts. Also a person's **decisions** may be founded in the present or perceived future positions, or yet based on facts occurred in the past. When a decision refers to a past existential position it may not affect reality, but may affect a person's thoughts about this same reality; and may also affect existential positions that may realize in the future. When a decision is based on a future existential position it may change those existential positions that come to reality.

3.2 – Evolution Theory

But everything that exists fits in the **natural order of things**. The biologist **Charles Darwin** in his **Evolution Theory** has indeed discovered a direction and sense for existence evolution. And his theory tells us that all beings evolve in a competition of capability and adaptability.

The Democratic Game and System Objective Theory accepts the idea that the biologist Charles Darwin in deed proved the very existence of God, when he discovered that life follows a natural evolution order in which all beings moves toward what is better and more adapted. Some God's deeds may be retraced through class equations, back in time to its origins. So evolutionism and creationism are perfectly integrated into the Objective Theory.

From there comes the **existential evolution principle** accepted by the objective theory: "Existence Evolution implies greater adaptability and efficiency for species, costumes, and rule systems".

Today there is more and more acceptance of democratic principles and values as a fundamental means for people to achieve a prosperous and peaceful world. Notice that Democratic principles are fixed, known and universal.

04 Evolution Objectives

As existence evolves in time, it follows a track that lead to an abstract point in the future that we call **objective**.

Objective - is an existential position in the future that is coming to reality. We may say that actual position or present was simply an **objective** in the past; now it is a **reality**. But **future objective** is not realized yet. That means we may change, create, or simply let it happen. When we try to do this we are conducting our reality to an objective. We may or may not be successful.

We may classify objectives either **systemic** or **proper**:

1- Systemic Objective – is naturally embedded in the Democratic Order in a given time, which in effect, dictates the way the rule system naturally evolves.

It is the **default objective** for any system; if nothing changes, things naturally go that way.

It does not depend, nor can be directly changed by any simple rule, but instead it is a result of the collective effect of all infinite existing commands in the Democratic Order itself.

The Democratic Order automatically forms a systemic objective that binds the rule system.

If we want to change **systemic objective**, we have to have the very Democratic Order that supports it, changed. But **Democratic Order** changes only if "**day to day reality**" changes.

There are innumerous ways according to which a "**day to day reality**" may change; for instance by new rules and respective enforcement, or better enforcement of existing rules. But these are not a matter for this book.

2- Proper Objective - is one that is established by an individual or collective **evolution planning**. They may occur in two classes; Evolutionary and Non-evolutionary.

2.1 - Evolutionary – or Darwinian - is one that confers greater adaptability and efficiency to people. For instance; "common good"

In spite of all uncertainty about future existential position, the **natural order of things** - that includes all natural principles - tells us that if we have a **democratic system**, then:

Only democratic principles make people individually and collectively pursue evolutionary objectives.

That is, if people are **sovereign of their system**, than all democratic principles must be present, for **evolutionary objectives to be pursued.**

2.2 - Non-evolutionary – or non Darwinian - is one that confers lesser adaptability and lesser efficiency to people; for instance; "imposed loss".

If we confront the concept of **non Darwinian** objective with the existential evolution principle, we conclude that non Darwinian objectives turn the very natural order of things, against those who pursue them. That means above all they endure, they have to face losses imposed by the natural order of things also. Notice that if evolution principle did not exist, it would be impossible for evolution objectives to be naturally fulfilled.

05 Evolution Planning

If we want to conduct reality to some specific future objective, we have to create and fulfill a **"proper evolution planning"** or simply **Evolution Planning**.

Evolution Planning is an "evolution abstract class object" that will lead reality to the decided objective. This must include; all intermediary class objects, methods, functions, and resources necessary for the context in which the desired objective will realize and of course to realize the desired object itself.

Intermediary Objects are things to be realized before that we want to realize. **Methods** are appropriate ways to realize them. That includes functions and resources. **Functions** are the appropriate capabilities and curse of actions. **Resources** are the necessary energy in any form to be mobilized and converted into the **reality** we want to appear.

If we want to change our **reality** to such an **objective**; then we have to project our thoughts and decisions into the future; than realize all abstract class objects necessary for that objective we want, to be fulfilled. The following figure 24 lustrates this concept:

Evolution Planning

```
Sovereignty
Mental
Nature                              Thoughts
Society
        History   Reality
Rule
    P            A          B              F

        Past    Present    Future
```

In this **"abstract class object of an evolution planning"** we find reality in the present; thoughts and decision advanced in the future. Notice that we have only positive thoughts, "for realizations" to be good.

Hence, we perceive the importance of a **more efficient environment**, where democratic characteristics are present. If this is not the case than an important part of our energy shall be spent literally **"paying imposed losses"** derived from system deficiencies. But "we should never give up our dreams!"

Notice that:

    a- As Darwinian objectives may be desirable and pursuable, by a majority of people, then they may make existential track toward a "better future", the shortest, smoothest, and least imponderable.

b- As Non-Darwinian objectives may realize "real class objects" that are desirable and pursuable, only by a handful of agents and undesirable by a relevant number of others, then they may create a track to the future that is more imponderable, twisty and cyclical.

c- Evolutionary or non-evolutionary objectives must be contained in the **systemic objectives** of a system. If that does not occur than they **do not realize**, except if they themselves **change reality**.

06 Evolution Values

What really drives evolution planning is value change. Everyone wants to create value; be it through new capabilities, materials and technology or via simple appropriation of other people's attributes or opportunities.

As we have already seen **Actual Value** corresponds to value by which operations are being realized in a given market and moment. Thus, relations are the appropriate means for creating value in any market system.

By other side, when market relations occur among participants of the same rule system, democratic characteristics affect only its participants and may not be an issue. But when market relations occur among participants of different rule systems, the level of democratic characteristics present in their respective systems become an issue to be seriously considered. We discuss some important phenomena that affect relations in the coming chapters of this book, among them; differentiation, dependent markets, quality, Qualitativity and objective polices.

07 Practical application

1 - Job Change

Let us analyze the following practical application for **evolution dynamics** concepts:

Consider that one day (time=0) one agent decided he should change his actual salary (S0) in his actual job (J0) by a new salary (S1) in another job (J1). He decided this because of the compensatory difference between salaries in his actual job and the new one (J1-J0 = D1). And he perceived he would have to educate himself in the new profession (go from E0 to E1), get government license to work on it (go from G0 to G1), and finally get the new job in the market to accomplish his goal (go from J0 to J1).

We call his actual situation by **position**; we call his actions to accomplish his goals by **dispute** and we call his objectives as **Advantage**. The following table figure 25 explains his position and dispute:

Evolution Process					
Evolution Time	Rule Salary	Society Job	Government License	Mental Education	Sovereign Decision
T0	S0	J0	L0	E0	D0
T1	S0	J0	L0	E0	D1
T2	S0	J0	L0	E1	D1
T3	S0	J0	L1	E1	D1
T4	S0	J1	L1	E1	D1
T5	S1	J1	L1	E1	D1

In each line we find the situation of the agent's attributes as time goes by.

Notice that column time refers to the moment each environment value is completed. Time five means the advantage is obtained. The time lapse between time zero and time five may be any time that is needed. For instance three years, five years, ten years etc...

What activated the sovereign environment agent's decision to produce actions to change reality, was a difference in salaries (slary0 – salary1) of (4, 000 – 1, 000 =) 3, 000 dollars. This advantage was the motive for all the actions.

Notice that:

a- The last aspect to be changed was the one the agent wanted to change in the beginning. Before that, he had to change all others in superior ranking classes.

b- If something goes wrong or is miscalculated in any of the environments and the necessary value is not or cannot be produced than the agent will fail to get his objective done; for example, if he does not get the job desired because there is no job left in the market in that position he wants.

c- A government program to improve a social-democratic class income must start somehow "improving" society "**offer**" to what he intends to improve "**demand**" for. Otherwise class (demand) will simply drive class (prices) down in that social-democratic class and **his goal will not be accomplished.** But notice that government does not rule directly over society. Because of this, naturally only indirect measures could be taken to improve offer; what should take a long time.

Additional Problems in Deficient Systems

Suppose this agent who wants a job change, actuates in a deficient system where aspect values, change over time.

Let us consider that when the agent started this dispute, he intended to gain an advantage of 3.000 dollars. But by the time he accomplished it, the advantage was only 800 dollars. This may be even **below motivation** level; that is, if it were like this in the beginning there could be no dispute at all. We call this phenomenon **advantage loss** or **motivation loss**. When we consider that this agent completed all evolution process intending to get an advantage of 3.000 and he ended up gaining only 800 dollars in advantage, we may say he was **inefficient in his objectives**. That is why it is very difficult for anyone to be efficient in a system that is inefficient or deficient, exactly because one never knows what future holds.

Any one may end up actuating inefficiently or deficiently in a system that is inefficient or deficient.

The longer it is to obtain a desired advantage, the greater it is the risk for **advantage loss**. That means when you are dealing with inefficient or deficient systems short time lapses must be preferred for any new project.

08 Cartesian Representation of Life Environment

Conceptually in a democratic government system, we may represent Life Environment in three sets of Cartesian axis bound together in present (time=0). The following figure 26 illustrates this:

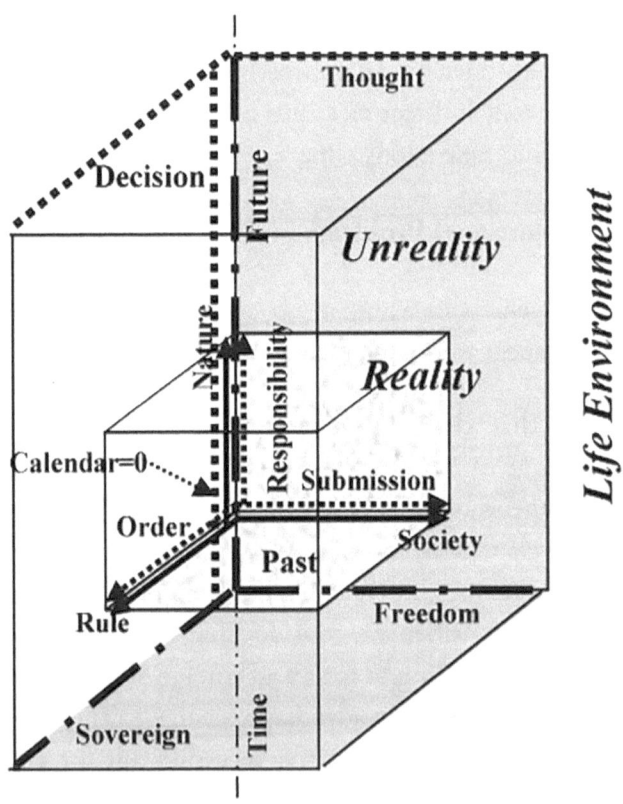

Notice that the natural order of things distributes these Cartesian axes as follows:

1- Time defines curse of Nature
2- Calendar defines Responsibility
3- Freedom defines Thought
4- Sovereign defines Decision
5- Rule defines Order

Society defines Submission

CHAPTER 12

DEMOCRATIC DIFFERENTIATION

01 Difference Treatment

Differences constitute a foundation for existence of all being and things. Without them materialization would not be possible. So being, they will never go away; and even they may be considered as an intrinsic characteristic of the very existence.

By another side, if we observe reality, we may clearly perceive people's worries with differences that exist in other people. Existing differences in other people tease or please observers.

They cause imbalanced thoughts to appear in the mental environment of observers, which we call "differential needs". These, "differential needs" give context to the appearance of other thoughts and decisions in the direction of attenuating them, which we call "differential thinking". Observers try to figure out what they can do, to profit from, to stand with, or even extinguish the existing differences in other people.

We may observe in history, that people's relations with different ones, have evolved through time. For instance, in the past some powerful people, protected, exterminated or submitted to slavery other weaker different people or persons they dealt with. Today this would be considered "inhuman" behavior.

Thus we perceive that evolution of all that exists, naturally has made thoughts, decisions and actions with respect to dealing with different people to change over time. And certainly it will continue to change.

Therefore that evolution is slow, gradual, and ordered by fixed universal rules. In other words they do not occur from night to day and are not established in a random fashion.

Thus, we shall always find participants in government rule systems, taking proper measures to face up all kinds of differences in a way they think is more appropriate. But in democratic systems all such actions conceptually need to conform to democratic characteristics and naturally they assume an objective nature. Because of this, we are able to study them in a way that is separated, from any personal opinion; exactly in their objective nature.

02 Democratic differentiation (in the rules)

Democratic Differentiation - is a process that introduces changes in aspects and values, of the democratic environment, caused by **active differentiator factors.**

Difference – is a generic title for the value that is absent or is in excess in a considered situation in real democratic environment that is caused by **differentiator factor's** actuations results; we also call **compensation**.

A democratic environment in any given moment has infinite aspects with respective values. After a dedifferentiation process there are still the same infinite aspects but with different relative values. Thus, a differentiation process affects relative values in all infinite aspects of a democratic environment.

This occurs because of the value conversion principle that states; "any value in any aspect may be converted to value in other aspect of the democratic environment". Exactly because of this principle, a difference introduced only in one aspect will affect all aspects of the democratic environment.

03 Difference Classification

A differentiation process may occur in one of two forms:

1- Selective Differentiation
2- Systemic Differentiation

But because of the **value conversion principle**, whenever there is one type of differentiation also there is the other type. In this chapter we will analyze selective differentiation.

04 Selective Differentiation

Selective Differentiation – is a process that creates value differences in some aspects of a proper rule system as a result of imbalanced actions put forward by someone who has the power and authority to do so. **Differential actions** are actions used in selective differentiation processes. The following figure 27 illustrates a selective differentiation process:

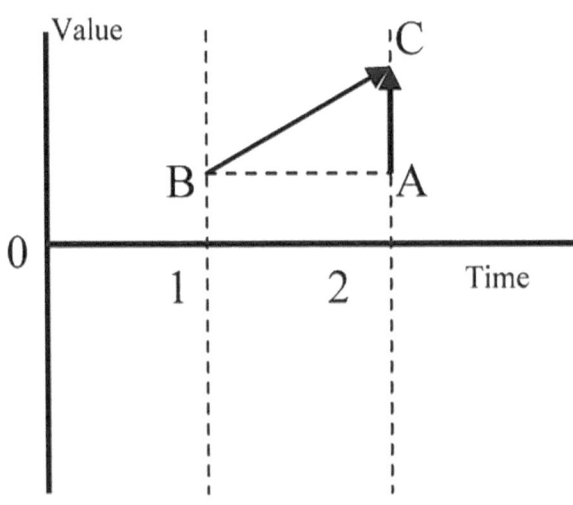

The differential action BC caused the appearance of difference AC.

05 Characteristics of Selective Differentiation

1. **Nature** – selective differentiation may be positive or negative

2. **Cause** – It is caused by direct differential action of authorities or a person who is able to do so.

3. **Occurrence** – selective differentiation presents it self totally in the rule environment. Selective differentiation is formed in people's thoughts. Then socially it enters the system, through people's vote on Election Day. Then it assumes a system objective conceptual dimension through rules. Then it assumes an actuating dimension through enforcement. Then it gets to the consequent dimension trough results. Then it passes on to day to day dimension where it interacts with other real phenomenon to form reality with differences.

4. **Control** – selective differentiation may be totally controlled by authorities.

5. **Formation** – selective differentiation is formed trough rules and values of the proper rule system.

6. **Expression** - as it is integrally contained in the rule system it may be expressed simply through **objective equations**. But it also may be expressed through **class equations** that show the **imponderable factor** responsible for its existence.

7. **Reach** – a selective differentiation deals exclusively with one selected class of agents and attributes. As a consequence reaches only a limited number of aspects.

8. **Context** – it works independently from any democratic situation that may exist in the democratic environment. This faculty

makes it a perfect weapon for imbalanced intervention on the rule system by aggressive authorities.

9. **Collateral** – Selective differentiation produces Systemic Differentiation as a collateral effect that reaches all infinite aspects of the democratic environment.

06 Tools

Actuating agents may use their exclusive power to create and operate any subsystem they wish to cause an intended selective differentiation in a certain class of consequent agents. In this work we shall refer only to three government tools 1- Tax Leverage; 2- Service Priority; 3- Aggressive Regulation.

6.1- Tax Leverage

Conceptually any democratic system must treat all participants equally. "All are equal toward the system". Because there is no classification of people in the conceptual definition of democracy; "democracy is government of people, by people, for people".

But in selective differentiation case authorities may classify system participants by any criteria they prefer; for instance by their respective social classes. And after that, they may impose a differentiated taxation as a function of these classes they have created with no relation to service delivered. The following class equations express this phenomenon:

$$\text{Classic: Tax}_{Pay} = \text{Tax}_{Average} + \text{T. Will}_{Controller}$$

$$\text{Supporter: Tax}_{Supporter} = \text{Tax}_{Average} + T_1 . \text{Will}_{Controller}$$

$$\text{Supported: Tax}_{Supported} = \text{Tax}_{Average} + T_2 . \text{Will}_{Controller}$$

$$\text{Total: } \sum \text{Tax}_{Pay} = \sum \text{Tax}_{Supporter} + \sum \text{Tax}_{Supported}$$

Where: T_{Pay} is the tax value to be effectively paid to authorities; $T_{Average}$ is the average taxation due to be paid by each participant; T, T_1, T_2 is a tax that is added or subtracted according to controller's will; $Will_{Controller}$ is an imponderable factor that represents will and power of controller to impose tax differentiation (Active=1; Inactive=0); $Tax_{Supporter}$ is the tax value to be paid by the supporters; $Tax_{Supported}$ is the tax value to be paid by the supported.

Leverage Indicators

To evaluate leverage we use three indicators that are: Leverage Indicator, Taxation Tension Indicator, and unitary leverage indicator.

Leverage Indicator - tells us how much is being paid above the average tax payment that is due to each agent.

$$\text{Leverage Indicator} = (T_{Pay}) / (T_{Average})$$

Taxation Tension Indicator - tells us the amount of tax paid by supporters with relation to what is paid by supported.

$$\text{Taxation Tension Indicator} = \sum Tax_{Supporter} / \sum Tax_{Supported}$$

Unitary Leverage indicator – tells us the necessary gain to classify as unitary in the leverage indicator. Their equations are as follows:

$$\text{Unitary Leverage indicator} = (T_{Average}) / x$$

Where; x is the average tax rate. Tax Leverage may be classified as; 1- **Negative** – when a person receives value from the system instead of paying; 2- **Decimal** – when the value paid to the system is lower than the tax average; **Unitary** – when the value paid to the system is equal to the tax average; **Supra-Decimal** – when the value paid to the system is higher than the tax average.

Inefficient or deficient systems work with very high leverage for supporters, high taxation tension and high unitary leverage indicators.

6.2- Service Priority

It consists in the democratic classification of system participants, followed by differentiated service offering as a function of these classes. The following class equations express this phenomenon:

$$\text{Classic: } S_{Received} = S_{Common} + S \cdot \text{Will}_{Controller}$$

$$\text{Supporter: } S_{Supporter} = S_{Common} + S_1 \cdot \text{Will}_{Controller}$$

$$\text{Supported: } S_{Supported} = S_{Common} + S_2 \cdot \text{Will}_{Controller}$$

$$\text{Total: } \Sigma S_{Received} = \Sigma S_{Supporter} + \Sigma S_{Supported}$$

Where: $S_{Received}$ is the service effectively received from authorities; S_{Common} is the common service due to each participant; S, S_1, S_2 is a service that is added or subtracted according to controller's will; $\text{Will}_{Controller}$ is an imponderable factor that represents will of controller to impose an aggressive service differentiation (Active=1; Inactive=0). $S_{Supporter}$ is the service value to be delivered to the supporters; $S_{Supported}$ is the service value to be delivered to the supported.

Priority Indicators

The priority indicator tells us how much is being delivered in services above of below the common services that are due to each agent. It is as follows:

$$\text{Priority Indicator} = (S_{Received}) / (S_{Common})$$

A **priority** may be; 1- **Decimal** – when the value delivered by the system is lower than the common service value; **Unitary** – when the value delivered by the system is equal to the common service value;

Supra-Decimal – when the value delivered by the system is greater than the common service value.

Inefficient or deficient systems work with very high priority for supported and very low priority for supporters.

6.3- Aggressive regulation

Consist on the approval and enforcement of aggressive rules that cause gains to certain classes and losses to others; we call them support systems. Through aggressive rules authorities may impose selective differentiation directly into the democratic environment day to day dimension. The integrate support systems.

We call support system to a set of aggressive rules that intend to collect imbalanced value and distribute it to other people.

A support system wave may be created by aggressive regulation according to the following class rank.

    0- Class (Support System)
    1- Subclass (Imbalanced Taxation)
    2- Subclass (Supporter – who will pay more taxes; T_1)
    2- Subclass (Supported – who will pay less taxes; T_2)
    1- Subclass (Imbalanced Services)
    2- Subclass (Supporter – who will receive less services; S_1)
    2- Subclass ((Supported – who will receive more services; S_2)

General support system class equation:

$$\sum \text{Tax}_{Pay} = \sum S_{Received} + \text{Repression}$$

So being, repression is a cost for the Class (Supported) who receive the imbalanced services. That is precisely why supported people in deficient systems want to reduce the value paid to repressors so that they may win more value for themselves. And for this reason, government technicians in deficient or inefficient systems are constantly under attack from politicians, from market players, and from people themselves; most of them supported. And authorities resort to "tax reclusions" to reduce their repressive costs.

Support Indicators

The **Transfer Efficiency** indicator tells us how much is being transferred as subsidy services with relation to what is being paid.

$$\text{Transfer Efficiency} = \sum S_{Received} / \sum Tax_{Pay}$$

The **Imbalance Indicator** tells us how much one supporter pays with relation to what he receives, or how much one supported receives with relation to what he pays.

$$\text{Imbalance Indicator}_{Supporter} = Tax_{Supporter} / S_{Supporter}$$
$$\text{Imbalance Indicator}_{Supported} = S_{Supported} / Tax_{Supported}$$

6.4 – Articulation Effect

If a support system has the same number of supporters and supported, than the supported will get the value paid less repression. But if there is a different number of supported, than each one will get an equal percentage of the value paid less repression; as indicated in the equation below.

$$S_{Supported} = (T_{Supporter} - \text{Repression}) \cdot N_{Supporter} / N_{Supported}$$

But the factor ($N_{Supporter} / N_{Supported}$) is a function of articulation. The following table figure 28 shows articulation effect on transfer efficiency indicator considering that there is no repression being applied.

Articulation%	Supporter	Supported	Effect
1	99	1	99
2	98	2	49
3	97	3	32
4	96	4	24
5	95	5	19
10	90	10	9
20	80	20	4
30	70	30	2.3
40	60	40	1.5
50	**50**	**50**	**1.0**
60	40	60	0.7
70	30	70	0.4
80	20	80	0.3
90	10	90	0.11
92	8	92	0.09
95	5	95	0.05
98	2	98	0,02

As we observe on the table an articulation of 50% is neutral toward the transfer indicator; below it the indicator increases and above it the indicator decreases. An articulation of 1% multiplies the value of transfer efficiency indicator by 99. While an articulation of 98% multiplies by 0.05; that means transfer efficiency indicator will be 5% or less. As articulation grows higher, without any increase in taxation, transfer efficiency tends to zero.

6.5 – Deviation Effect

If we consider a support system for a specific purpose than all that is not going to that objective class is considered to be deviation.

Deviation in a support system is a value that is delivered to other than its main purpose.

When we take deviation into consideration the equation for service received by the supported, stays like this:

$$S_{Supported} = (T_{Supporter} - \text{Repression} - \text{Deviation}) \cdot N_{Supporter} / N_{Supported}$$

Highly articulated systems may offer lowest quality services possible to the personal supported while presenting high repression and high deviation. That tells us support systems are excellent options for solidarity only systems, but very poor options for high articulations and deviations subsidy systems.

6.6 – Numerical example (in dollars)

Let us suppose the following values for a support system that will do a selective differentiation required on election result.

$T_{Average} = 600$
$Service_{Common} = 600$
$T_1 = + 2,000$
$T_2 = - 500$
$S_1 = - 400$
$S_2 = + 1,500$

Class equation for tax payment is this:
$Tax_{Supporter} = Tax_{Average} + T_1 \cdot Will_{Controller}$
$Tax_{Supporter} = 600 + 2,000 \cdot Will_{Controller} = 2,600$
$Tax_{Supported} = 600 - 500 \cdot Will_{Controller} = 100$

Class equation for service is as follows:
$Service_{Received} = Service_{Common} + S \cdot Will_{Controller}$
$Service_{Supporter} = 600 - 400 \cdot Will_{Controller} = 200$
$Service_{Supported} = 600 + 1,500 \cdot Will_{Controller} = 2,100$

Indicators are as follows:

Leverage Indicator $_{Supporter}$ = 2.600/600 = 4.33
Leverage Indicator $_{Supported}$ = 100/600 = 0.16
Priority Indicator $_{Supporter}$ = 200 / 600 = 0.33
Priority Indicator $_{Supported}$ = 2100 / 600 = 3.5
Transfer Efficiency = 2,100/ 2,600 = 0.80
Imbalance Indicator $_{Supporter}$ = 2,600/ 200 = 13
Imbalance Indicator $_{Supported}$ = 2,100/ 100 = 21

07 Consequences of Selective Differentiation

7.1 – Substantial value leverage for Politicians

One of the substantial consequences of support systems is the electoral leverage they present for politicians. The following example illustrates this thought:

Consider we have a class of workers, integrated by 10,000 government employees receiving a salary of just 1,000 dollars each one per month.

Now let us calculate the impact of a support system to discount from this class 1% to 75% of their salaries every month, and distribute it away freely to poor people in the form of 50 dollars subsidy per person per month. The following table figure 29 shows these calculations;

Support System ; Supporters = 10,000; Salaries = 1,000 /month					
1	2	3	4	5	6
1%	100,000	50	2,000	-8,000	-1
3%	300,000	50	6,000	-4,000	0
5%	500,000	50	10,000		0
6%	600,000	50	12,000	2,000	0
7%	700,000	50	14,000	4,000	0
9%	900,000	50	18,000	8,000	1
11%	1,100,000	50	22,000	12,000	1
13%	1,300,000	50	26,000	16,000	2
15%	1,500,000	50	30,000	20,000	2
20%	2,000,000	50	40,000	30,000	3
25%	2,500,000	50	50,000	40,000	4
30%	3,000,000	50	60,000	50,000	5
35%	3,500,000	50	70,000	60,000	6
40%	4,000,000	50	80,000	70,000	7
45%	4,500,000	50	90,000	80,000	8
50%	5,000,000	50	100,000	90,000	9
55%	5,500,000	50	110,000	100,000	10
60%	6,000,000	50	120,000	110,000	11
65%	6,500,000	50	130,000	120,000	12
70%	7,000,000	50	140,000	130,000	13
75%	7,500,000	50	150,000	140,000	14

Legend:
1 – Percent over gain discount
2 – Total Collected
3 - Subsidy
4 – Number of those supported
5 – Votes Supposedly Gained Net
6 – Electoral Leverage

As we may see, when such support system discounts 55% from the supporter class, who earn only 1,000 dollars to give it in the form of 50 dollars free subsidy to supported people, it produces to the controllers 100,000 votes. That is 10 times more votes than what is lost in the process. If their salaries are 20.000 dollars all these values would be multiplied by more than 20.

If we consider that 10, 000 people with a salary of 20 thousand dollars per month is submitted to a discount of 55% in their salaries. That gives support system controllers the amount of 110 million dollars in imbalanced tax collected. This may be distributed as a 50 dollar per month, subsidy to 2.2 million electors, reaching an electoral leverage, of 220.

7.2 – Other substantial value leverages

We call corporate agents those who run corporation waves (socially called corporations). These agents may receive any amount of money, support system controllers may want to deliver to them under any title, such as; subsidy, incentive, compensation, premium, bail out or other.

Most of public accountant systems do not distinguish between expenditure and investment. All these are considered as investment. So being, authorities may expend supporter's money to do whatever expenses they may wish to do. For instance; they may build exuberant palaces for themselves, exuberant installations for some events, construct roads or bridges to nowhere.

7.3 – Other substantial losses

When a worker gets his salary from his employer, he gets the best value for it. But when the employer hands the money to government, and this one hands out subsidy for every supported; possibly the worker will get only a fraction of his work due value.

By other side when poor people get fraternity or solidarity from a government, they get the most possible value they may get. But when government simply takes money away from supporters to give to supported, poor people will probably get only a fraction of that value; because they will be included in a Class (Personal Supported) that is much bigger than theirs.

7.4 – Quality change

Let us consider a Democratic Situation Graphic Indicator for a certain democratic environment. This indicator shows us a democratic environment Profile in the aspect we choose. The following figure 30 shows an illustrative representation of this indicator.

It was assembled as follows:
  a- All participants of the democratic environment ware aligned side by side.
  b- They were sorted in crescent order of personal gains.
  c- They were divided into five classes of equal number o people, called strips.
  d- These strips of people ware stack one on top of the other

Thus, we have an abstract class object that represents a real class environment, and allows us to study some of its characteristics with relation to considered aspects.

Let us analyze what happens when through selective differentiation, an authority moves an agent Class (A), from Strip 4 to Strip 2, in personal gain aspect; and a group of agents Class (B) from Strip 1 to Strip 2 also in personal gain aspect. Let us say authorities have used exclusive state power for that, and also they made sure there was no economic loss or gain for the environment as a whole, stemming from this process.

Quality Loss - As a consequence Class (A) will lose his democratic and social situation with relation to friends, neighbors, partners, and other classes; while Class (B) will gain. But "gain aspect" is directly correlated to "consumption aspect" in the democratic environment. Let us take a look in what happens in the consumption aspect. The following figure 30 shows this:

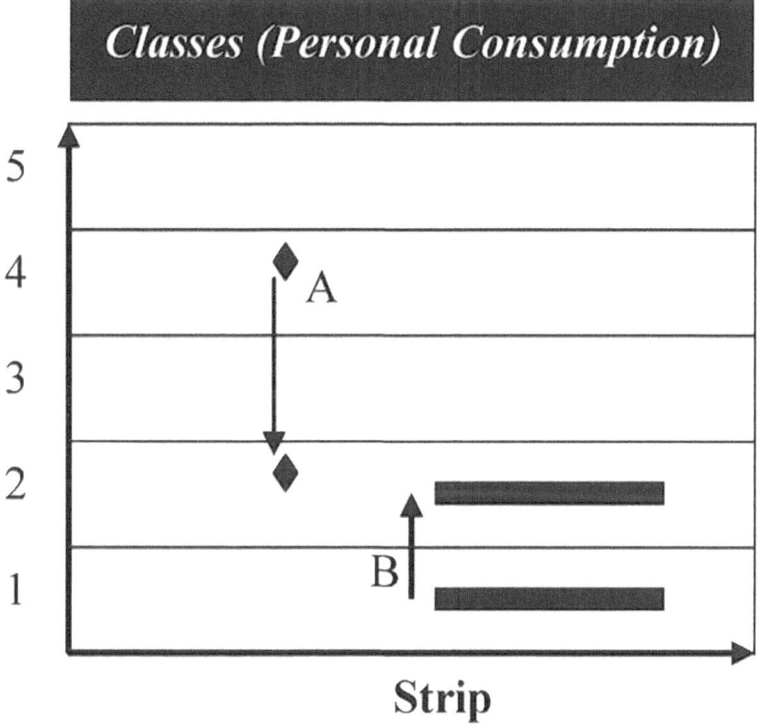

Strip

In this graph the loss of acquisitive power for Class (A) is evident. Class (A) will consume products and services that are typical of Class (Strip 2). In economic terms there is no change in overall value because what is lost in consumption by Class (A) is gained by Class (B). Therefore as Class (A) stopped consuming products and services typical of Class (Strip 4) and passed to consume products that are typical of Class (Strip 2), this quality gap was not balanced in the process. That means a loss in demand for more technologically advanced products may be occurring in this environment; and they may either be sold abroad for any value or simply be extinguished.

But now let us consider an authority did the inverse movement and heightened Class (A) from Strip 2 to Strip 4; and lowered Class (B) from Strip 2 to Strip 1.

Quality Gain – Although conceptually there is no loss or gain in economic value, in the democratic environment there is a gain in quality of consumption; because Class (A) changes its habits to include technologically more advanced products typical of Class (Strip 4).

That is why authorities in more efficient systems naturally worry the most about protecting medium class gains; people in needy may receive a greater amount of solidarity (donation of public resources approved by the great majority of participants); and fraternity actions (voluntary social donation of private resources to those in needy), may complement solidarity in directing resources to people in needy.

Selective differentiation class wave generates consequent waves that we shall consider in the next chapter Systemic differentiation.

CHAPTER 13

SYSTEMIC DIFFERENTIATION

Systemic Differentiation – is the process that creates value differences in all aspects of a democratic system as a result of existing imbalances in the **existential environment** with relation to the **natural order of things**, which force the democratic environment into change.

01 Graphic Representation of Systemic Differentiation

The following figure 31 shows the result of a hypothetic systemic differentiation process:

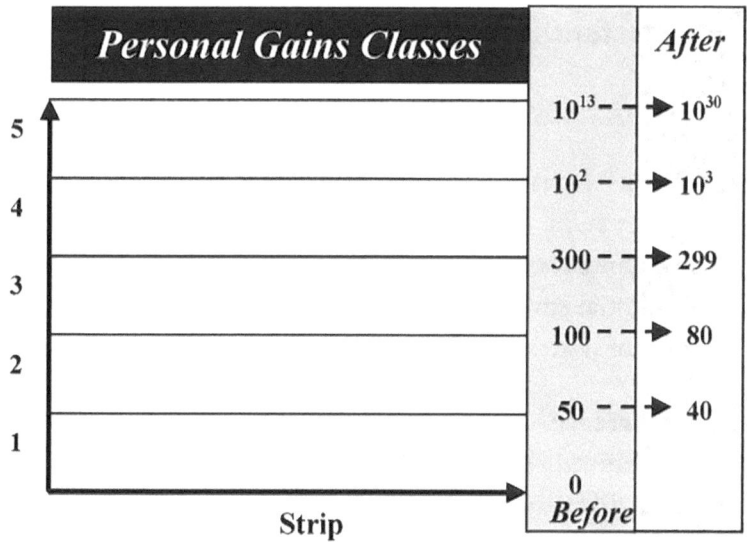

This is a **Democratic Situation Graphic Indicator** put together as before, but with values in the right side of the figure referring to the highest gain in the stripe in two different times - before the differentiation process and after it has occurred.

Notice that the highest value in each stripe has changed. This difference is exactly the result of the systemic differentiation process.

Comparing the numbers notice that: the stripe 1 had its maximum gain altered from 50 to 40 monetary units; that means their agents lost democratic situation. On stripe 2 notice that its maximum gain was altered from 100 to 80 monetary units; their agents also lost democratic situation. On stripe 3, notice that its maximum gain was lightly altered from 300 to 299 monetary units. On stripe 4, maximum gain had a positive variation from 10^2 to 10^3 monetary units. On stripe 5 notice that maximum gain had the greater positive variation from 10^{13} to 10^{30} monetary units; their agents gained democratic situation.

This is a classical example of a systemic differentiation process that causes **gain concentration** in the democratic environment.

02 Characteristics

1. **Nature** – systemic differentiation may be positive or negative.

2. **Cause** – Imbalances in any existence environment with respect to the natural order of things may be its motivation. That is, any imbalance formed in any of the 5 environments that compound existential environment may cause a contextual reaction in the form of systemic differentiation; for instance, a "society taboo".

3. **Occurrence** – when prices appear diminished in the democratic environment systemic differentiation is expressed as a **social value difference** that is subtracted from values in the democratic environment. When prices appear with increased value in

the democratic environment then systemic differentiation is expressed as a **democratic value difference**.

Example; investors, that demand high government yields to compensate themselves for deficiencies that may exist in the government system.

Notice that **social value differences** generally pass unnoticed by all accountant methods in use today.

4. **Control** – systemic differentiation cannot be controlled by authorities of the proper rule system. But reality agents that make them happen – including, proper rule, social, and natural agents - may have some influence over it.

   Notice that natural agents include natural phenomena such as rain, thunderstorm, hurricane etc.

5. **Formation** – systemic differentiation is put forward without any proper rule. It changes day to day reality, and consequently changes the entire rule system altering until its very democratic order.

6. **Expression** - Due to the fact that, it is a class phenomenon, rather than, an objective phenomenon, only **class equations** make it possible to correctly express its occurrence.

7. **Reach** – conceptually a systemic differentiation reaches all aspects of the democratic environment – and directly affects all participants. The Lirian Method of Objective Democratic Evaluation – MLIRA, allows us to measure the effects of systemic differentiation in as many aspects as we may want to.

8. **Context** – it produces its effects in tune with existing democratic situation at each aspect. It affects differently, each different aspect and social classes.

9. **Collateral** – systemic differentiation may give reason for installation by authorities of subsequent, preventive, or reactive **selective differentiation** processes.

03 Important causes for Systemic Differentiation

Conceptually any internal or external cost causes systemic differentiation. But by far the most important source of systemic differentiation, are the imponderable costs against participants, which ones function as imponderable factors that introduce diverse objective internal or external, Subclass (Cost) objects from the differentiation idea- Class (Differentiation).

Imponderable costs against participants may destroy values in all democratic system aspects and yet not be noticed. We say they work in the same way as body tension works in our human body; "they may kill the patient and not give a signal".

In this chapter we shall discuss some details about costs of; autocratic responsibility regimes; censored electoral decision; sovereign- submission; and selective differentiation.

04 Cost of autocratic responsibility regimes

These are costs stemming from responsibility regimes that impose losses to innocent people. To understand this concept let us discuss a few things about responsibility regimes.

4.1 – Responsibility Regime

Regime is conceptually a set of commands for establishing a value with relation to another.

Responsibility Regime is a relation between obligations and rights. Considering (A = obligations), and (B = rights), we have two different

responsibility regimes in the democratic environment: **Democratic Responsibility and Autocratic Responsibility.**

4.2 – Democratic Responsibility Regime

Democratic Responsibly Regime establishes that every participant must be responsible for the expenses he causes.

In this case: A= B

We call this relation efficient equilibrium because it is reached with no imposed loss to any other participant.

In the Efficient State Model a variation of this regime called more efficient equilibrium is used. Under a more efficient responsibility regime all participants must even their relations with the government system within a certain time period that is adjusted to allow all necessary system tasks to be satisfactorily fulfilled – such as 50 years for instance. For instance, a child (future participant), that need government help, could pay back as a participant, in the same way he received that help, thus not involving other participants in their parents irresponsibility or miss fortune.

This conceptually allows the government system to perform any curse of actions necessary in a day to day life, in a more efficient and more adapted way. This regime depends upon an objective and logical equilibrium that can be simply expressed to all participants.

4.3 – Autocratic Responsibility Regime

Autocratic Responsibly Regime establishes that every participant must be responsible for expenses according to authority's decision.

That means in systems that use this responsibility regime, there is an authority that is officially able to tell who is responsible for what. We also call these regimes as Irresponsibility Regimes; because, they do not attend to democratic principles. Or else we may call them Just Regimes, because they use "just equilibrium" to relate obligations and rights.

In this case: $A \neq B$

We call this relation **just equilibrium** because it is reached with imposed losses, or attributing gains, to some participants. Just equilibrium is defined in class equation as follows:

$$A = B_{Just}$$

$$B_{Just} = B + B_J . \text{Will}_{Authority}$$

Where:

B_{Just} is the just value of B

B is the rights value that is equal to obligation A

B_J is an **objective factor** introduced by the imponderable factor.

$\text{Will}_{Authority}$ – is the imponderable factors (active=1; inactive=0), that introduces the objective factor in the equation.

As "A" is different from B_{Just}, then no none can say what obligations creates what rights. All depends on the authority will. The following figure shows the differences between these two responsibility regimes.

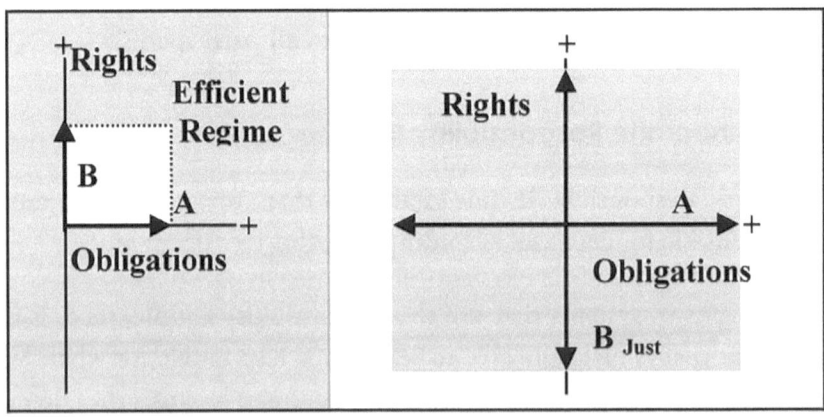

As we may see in the figure, in efficient regimes, knowing the value of rights is enough to tell the obligations value; or vice versa. This is not a source of instability to the system.

But in a just regime, it is not possible to know what the rights are, even if we know the value of obligations. Both of them are represented in the figure by spectrums where authority may decide where to place their values. This may cause instability and imposed losses in the proper rule system because every one may pressure to increase the rights he is interested in, and decrease obligations at the same time.

Just equilibrium is used in systems that use Just State Model formation, which one does not hold democratic characteristics on its relation with participants.

4.4 – Existence Just Equilibrium

When authority cause an imbalance to occur in the rule environment, in order to achieve what he intends as just equilibrium, he causes an imbalance to occur in the existential environment.

Notice that the proper rule system is not isolated in reality or in existence; quite in the contrary it is integrated with all other systems. We separate them for analyses purpose only.

So, whenever an imbalance (positive or negative) occurs in any of the 5 existential environments – reality plus unreality - the natural order of things provides imbalance waves that reestablish a new just equilibrium, which may present itself in the rule environment as systemic differentiation. Because of this, values may move from one environment to another environment within reality or unreality - for instance from rule environment to social environment. Or else they can simply be made un-disposable in the same environment.

By other side Evolution Principle states that; "existence evolves for a more efficient and more adapted situation in the future".

That means agent classes in compliance with evolution principles, when fulfilling their objectives, are able to count on the natural order of things in their favor. And agent classes that are not in compliance with evolution principles, when fulfilling their objectives, face the natural order of things pressure against them - in order to make them comply with it, or simply vanish.

That is the way an existence just balance is reached by natural order of things. So existence just balance is obtained by the very natural order of things in a way that favors those who comply with evolution principles

Considering that in real democratic systems we will always find a number of people that do not comply with the natural order of things for various reasons, than we may say that; "perfect democratic systems will continue forever to be a utopia, due to existential characteristics and dynamics.

05 Cost of censored electoral decision

These are costs stemming from imposed losses or lost opportunities that are hidden to censored participants. To understand this concept let us discuss a few things about a decision.

We cannot go to a move and also go to a beach or any other place at the same time. When we chose "go to a movie" we are giving up all other options that we could do, or go to, in that same time period.

Same thing occurs when we need to make a decision in the democratic system. Whenever we chose one track to follow through, we need to abandon all other tracks at our disposal. Therefore, each decision in the democratic environment hides in itself a gain or loss of opportunity concerning to each one of the abandoned aspects – that were not chosen.

That means when we have to make a decision in the democratic environment we have to consider all options at our disposal and chose the best one. We cannot simply decide to continue doing what we have done in the past because **this may lead to opportunity loss**. Otherwise, if we chose the best option, we will be realizing an opportunity gain and complying with the existence evolution principle. Any other option that we chose will carry a **decision cost**. To accomplish this, we do need **freedom** to be a rule principle in the democratic system.

Censored electoral decision costs reduce disposable value for all participants in the democratic system, and changes relative value in its infinite aspects through systemic differentiation processes. Then, in order to avoid decision cost appearance, we need to guarantee that **plain freedom** is present in the democratic system.

Deficient or inefficient systems do not use freedom as a basic principle, and this causes them to operate with very high **censored electoral decision cost.**

5.1 – Cost of Sovereign Submission

These are costs stemming from imposed losses or lost opportunities that are caused by authorities actuating as sovereign in place and against the will of participants. To understand this concept let us discuss a few things about sovereignty and submission.

Sovereignty is the power to decide things at last instance. **Submission** is acceptance of a sovereign decision.

By other side, as we know the objective theory accepts all proper rule system as democratic systems, with different levels of democratic characteristics. But it accepts only one concept for perfect democracy. This is: Democracy is a government of the people, by the people, for the people.

In a perfect democratic system sovereignty presents itself shared among all participants. But there are many real "democratic" systems where we find authorities deciding in the last instance about things. So being, participants become servers and servers become sovereigns of these real systems.

Servers-made-sovereigns may create and enforce laws that they themselves want; even against the will of participants. That configures a sovereign submission syndrome.

Because of this syndrome, decisions end up not being taken in the **sovereign environment** as they should, but instead they are taken in the **proper rule environment.** These costs are objectively generated when people do not want to fulfill authority's decisions. And some of these decisions are put down on Election Day.

The objective values they create reduce disposable value in the democratic environment, and affect all its infinite aspects through systemic differentiation processes. Deficient and Inefficient systems conceptually operate with very high sovereign submission costs.

06 Cost of Selective Differentiation

These are costs stemming from selective differentiation processes either against or in favor of participants. To understand this concept let us discuss a few things about selection processes themselves.

Any situation inside a real democratic environment has infinite aspects and coordinates. And these coordinates may flow from one aspect to the other, due to **value conversion principle**. This means we cannot alter a situation without altering all infinite aspects and coordinates of that situation in the democratic environment.

But selective differentiation, affects only a certain group of aspects in the democratic environment. And it is put forward by means of **pressure**. This pressure may assume the form of **exclusive state power**, or **exclusive market power**, or **exclusive technology** power, or any other thing that people cannot cope with; and that pressure end up moving the "real class object" in the selected direction, chosen by the controller of the process.

Therefore, in spite of the occurrence of a selective differentiation process, disposable value for all participants in the democratic system is not created. Indeed it is diminished by the exact amount of energy used to produce that differentiation process.

Thus we may say that; "whatever is added to one aspect has to be diminished from other aspects in the same or in other environments, in order to keep disposable value stable in the existence system". And we also may say that: "whatever is spent simply to force change in the environment is simply diminished from the system disposable value". All these infinite aspects alterations occur exactly through systemic differentiation. The following figure 33 shows a representation of a selective differentiation process and corresponding systemic differentiation process:

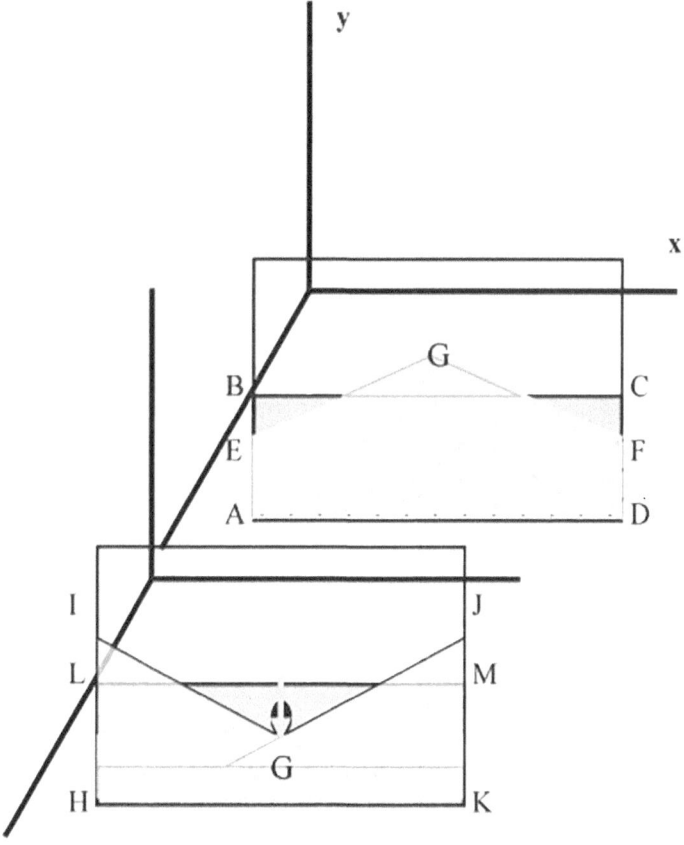

In this figure we considered a set of coordinates of various situations initially represented by line B to C, placed on the same level within a plan that is parallel to the plan formed by axis y and x. Figure (ABCD) or (HLMK).

Then, when we apply a **positive** selective differentiation process to coordinate G, taking it to a higher point above all others. The figure shows that as a result, a new configuration for that same set of points appear now represented by line E to G and to F. figure (AEGFD).

When we apply a **negative** selective differentiation to coordinate G, taking it to a lower point below all others; the figure shows that as a result, a new configuration for that same set of points appear now represented by line E to G and to F. figure (HIGJK).

In both cases (positive or negative) the result of a selective differentiation process is the movement of values in a greater then selected amount of aspects in the desired direction, and also the movement of values in all other infinite aspects of the democratic environment in the opposite direction to the one initially desired.

In other words, when we forcefully overvalue something in the rule environment, we end up overvaluing other things that we even did not want to, and at the same time we undervalue all other infinite aspects around us. All this occurs because selective differentiation by itself does not create value.

This study is just an introductory presentation of the phenomenon of imponderable costs against participants. Understanding them in a case by case basis may lead to the formation of a more efficient system; simply because it is from them that most of the objective costs are formed within the system through systemic differentiation.

07 Consequences of Systemic Differentiation

In chapter Autocratic Systems we have studied some actuating waves coming from autocratic aggressive actions. But we did not discuss anything about interactive class waves in that chapter. That is because it is indeed a very complex matter. A single set of actuating waves (class and imbalance waves), conceptually causes infinite interactive waves to be present. And each of them causes interactive class effects to appear in day to day dimension. In the next three chapters we shall discuss about some of these Interactive waves and their effects; how to identify and even measure them.

CHAPTER 14

DIFFERENTIAL INTERACTIVE WAVES

01 Differential Interactive Waves

Systemic waves never appear alone in the system, rather they appear as a wide spread phenomenon that reaches the entire proper rule environment. When there is one systemic differentiation wave, there are many others.

For example, if a "work done" is paid 100% of its real intrinsic value, then it shows there is no systemic differentiation wave present in this environment. Also, it does not say this, but conceptually there is no other systemic differentiation wave at all, in this proper rule environment. That means conceptually there is no systemic piracy market, interest rates are at its best value, and there is peace.

But consider another example where a "work done" is paid only 10% of its intrinsic value; this clearly shows that a "work market systemic differentiation wave" is present in this environment. Therefore, it does not say this, but in this same environment many other systemic differentiation waves are surely also present. For example, recorded music, print books, brand products; many of them probably are been sold as fake products in piracy markets; interest rates are very high; and violence may be rampant. We call these as Differential Interactive Waves.

Differential Interactive Waves

Differential Interactive Waves are classes of waves that also appear, or may appear, when any differentiation process is present in a proper rule system and also imposes differentiation values on it. Some of them may activate systemic differentiation; others may be consequence of its existence. Exactly because of differentiation interactive wave's activities: democratic markets in all environmental aspects increase, or reduce differentiation presence in its price as a whole according to each specific relation.

This is a **valuation principle**. Because of this principle no one is able to improve a situation by addressing only one or a group of its aspects. For instance, we cannot increase people's medium income simply by giving all people more education. Education needs jobs to produce value, and; if no jobs are appropriately created probably the same jobs, with the same income, shall be occupied any way; that is, conceptually keeping the medium income, right where it was before the education increase.

Let us suppose that a selective differentiation process continues increasing forever; then, all interactive waves will show up, in the day to day dimension of reality, as Interactive Class Effects.

Interactive Class Effects – constitute "real class objects" of interactive waves that may be observed in day to day reality, most of the time as disconnected phenomena. In this chapter we shall consider interactive waves and correspondent interactive class effects of; Secondary Assistance; and Differentiation Market. In the other two coming chapters we shall discuss Democracy Inefficiency, and Qualitativity.

02 Secondary Assistance Market

When government officials distribute assistance to a class of agents, we call that primary assistance, and those who receive it primary supported. The distribution of primary assistance to primary supported constitutes a market that we call Primary Assistance Market.

But, when someone receives primary assistance, he goes on somewhere, and buys something. That constitutes a market that we call Secondary Assistance Market.

In the secondary market we find products and gains in any form that we call Secondary Assistance. And those who receive secondary assistance we call secondary supported.

Thus, the money received in a primary assistance market, normally creates a dependent secondary assistance market. Whenever we have one, the other is also present; and when the primary assistance market disappears the secondary assistance market also disappears.

2.1 - Class Analysis

A government decides to create a support system, so it is a subclass of class government.

A support system is divided into subclasses tax collection, repression and assistance. As assistance delivered constitutes the primary assistance market, we may say that it is a subclass of support system.

But as we said primary assistance market creates secondary assistance market. Then secondary assistance market is a subclass of primary assistance market.

The class rank for these interactive waves stays as follows:

Rank

    0– Class (Government)
    1- Subclass (Support System)
    2- Subclass (Primary Assistance Market)
    3- Subclass (Primary Assistance)
    4- Subclass (Primary Supported)

    2- Subclass (Secondary Assistance market)
    3- Subclass (Products)

3- Subclass (Secondary Assistance)
4- Subclass (Secondary Supported)

Indeed, Secondary Assistance market, in its turn creates, a Third Assistance Market, and this one creates a Fourth Assistance Market and so forth; but in this text we shall consider only the secondary level.

2.2 - Class Equations

Class equation for primary assistance market:

$$\text{Tax. Will}_{\text{Authority}} = (\text{Repression} + \text{Assistance Market}_{\text{Primary}}) \text{Will}_{\text{Authority}}$$

That leads to:

$$[\text{Assistance Market}_{\text{Primary}} = (\text{Tax} - \text{Repression})]. \text{Will}_{\text{Authority}}$$

Notice that in class equations an imponderable factor that multiplies an expression, may introduce any objective factor in any isolated part of that expression. This propriety allows us to substitute all imponderable factors relating to the same subjective source by a single imponderable factor that multiplies the whole expression.

Class equation for secondary assistance market

$$\text{Assistance Market}_{\text{Secondary}} = \text{Material} + \text{Assistance}_{\text{Secondary}}$$

But class (Secondary Assistance) presents itself in various subclasses which in their turn have other subclasses. In this text we shall consider the following ones:

$$\text{Assistance}_{\text{Secondary}} = \text{Class (Work Pay)} + \text{Class (Application Returns)} + \text{Class (Taxes)}$$

$$\text{Classes (work pay)} = \text{Subclass (Poor)} + \text{Subclass (Medium)} + \text{Subclass (Rich)}$$

Class (Taxes) = Subclass (Local) + Subclass (State) + Subclass (Union)

Class equation for the whole support market

$$\text{Assistance Market}_{Secondary} = \text{Assistance Market}_{Primary}. \text{Will}_{Authority}$$

This mathematical analysis using class equations, shows us that all social and democratic classes involved in support systems, become subclasses of the authorities that control them.

Markets that are originated by another broader market exist; wile market conditions allow them to exist. But government markets exist only wile government wants them to exist. Secondary markets have their existence completely dependent upon the existence of the primary market that originated them, and they will never exist by themselves.

Authorities control everything in the primary market "by the stroke of their pen".

And authorities may influence the secondary market just as they decide things about the primary market structure.

For example, if they distribute primary assistance in form of products than they may determine the suppliers they want. But if authorities do not control of the primary market characteristics, than they cannot say anything about the secondary market, only their results may tell something.

2.3 - Numerical Example of Class (Support System)

The tables below show a numeric example of primary and secondary market assistance.

2.3.1 - Subclass (Primary Assistance Market)

Suppose an authority distributed 30 billion dollars in cash as follows:

That money was distributed to, and collected by, Class (Poor) in cash, what means it is a Class (Profit) for them. It affected 20 million persons in that class.

Every primary participant collected 1.5 thousand dollars to "make his living". That is 100% percent for that class.

Following Figure 34 shows this market.

Subclass (Primary Assistance Market)		
Primary Market Distribution		
Classes	*Value%*	*Billions*
Class (Products)		
Class (Tax)		
Class (Work)		
Class (Profit)	100%	30
Total Primary	100%	30
Primary Assistance Collected		
Classes	*Value%*	*Billions*
Class (Poor)	100%	30
Class (Medium)		
Class (Rich)		
Total Primary Assistance		30
Total Class (Products)		0
Affected Population Distribution		
Classes	*Population%*	*Millions*
Class (Poor)	100%	20
Class (Medium)		
Class (Rich)		
Total	100%	20
Individual Value Collected		
Classes	*Unit%*	*Unit*
Class (Poor)\	100%	1500
Class (Medium)\		
Class (Rich)\		
	100%	1.500

2.3.2 - Subclass (Secondary Assistance Market)

But this process creates a secondary market that will convert primary assistance to products and services. We suppose that this distribution occurred according to the following:

The secondary assistance is the value distributed to people in each social class, in form of profit, work pay, or any other form of monetary gain. As we have said, those who receive secondary assistance are classified as **secondary supported**. Figure 35 shows the value generated by the secondary market to each class.

"Products" means all social and rule value was excluded from this value. That is it is only the value of material being sold. It is conceptually relatively greater in raw material rich products, and relatively lower in technological advanced products.

It also shows population in each social class that was affected by this specific secondary market. As you may see most of the population affected is poor people.

Also, it shows the money collected in various forms, by each one in their classes.

Subclass (Secondary Assistance Market)

Secondary Market Distribution

Classes	Value%	Billions
Class (Products)	30%	9,00
Class (Tax)	30%	9,00
Class (Work)	25%	7,50
Class (Profit)	15%	4,50
Total Secondary	100%	30

Secondary Assistance Collected

Classes	Value%	Billions
Class (Poor)	30%	6,3
Class (Medium)	30%	6,3
Class (Rich)	40%	8,4
Total Secondary Assistance		21,00
Total Class (Material)		9,00

Affected Population Distribution

Classes	Population%	Millions
Class (Poor)	83,2%	50
Class (Medium)	16,6%	10
Class (Rich)	0,2%	0,1
Total	100,0%	60,1

Individual Value Collected (Dollars)

Classes		Dollars
Class (Poor)\	0,15%	126
Class (Medium)\	0,74%	630
Class (Rich)\	99,1%	84.000
	100%	84.756

Affected Population Relation

Classes by	Class (Medium)	Class (Rich)
Class (Poor)	5	500
Class (Medium)	1	100
Class (Rich)	0,01	1

As we see in this specific case every poor secondary participant went home with 126 dollars in their pockets; to buy things and constitute other dependent consumer market. Every medium secondary participant went home with 630 dollars that may be used to improve his social status; for instance, they may buy new homes, luxury cars or restaurants. And every rich secondary participant got 84 thousand dollars to grow their fortunes, and make them richer.

The value received by poor and even medium class people as secondary assistance is much lower than the value paid in primary assistance. This fact pressures people in these classes to become primary supported. That is precisely why many people quit their jobs just to receive primary assistance.

In this specific example; poor to rich population relation is very high. Also; medium to rich relation is very high. This explains why social differences grow, and medium and rich classes accept them, wherever they are used in the world. But of course, primary market structure may be defined by authorities in a way that it may smoothen these relations down; for instance, supplying most of the **primary assistance** in services or goods.

2.4 - Market Substitution Effect

When authorities collect taxes to fund a support system, they indeed kill a part or a whole market that may be funded just with that suppressed value. But when they distribute primary assistance, they create the secondary market. The following class equation explains this thought.

$$\text{Market}_{\text{Suppressed}} = \text{Market}_{\text{Secondary}} - \text{Repression}.$$

That means we shall have Market $_{\text{Suppressed}}$ (Taxes; Wages; Profits; Products) that may be substituted by Market $_{\text{Secondary}}$ (Taxes; Wages; Profits; Products). Also, that we have Market $_{\text{Suppressed}}$ (Local Tax; State Tax, Union Tax) that may be substituted by Market $_{\text{Secondary}}$ (Local Tax; State Tax, Union Tax). And we have a loss in that process represented by repression.

Let us consider that no repression is required for a specific support system. Then we may write the following class equations.

$$\text{Tax}_{\text{Suppressed}} = \text{Tax}_{\text{Secondary}} + D_{\text{Tax}} \cdot \text{Differences}$$

$$\text{Wage}_{\text{Suppressed}} = \text{Wage}_{\text{Secondary}} + D_{\text{Wage}} \cdot \text{Differences}$$

$$\text{Profit}_{\text{Suppressed}} = \text{Profit}_{\text{Secondary}} + D_{\text{Profit}} \cdot \text{Differences}$$

$$\text{Products}_{\text{Suppressed}} = \text{Products}_{\text{Secondary}} + D_{\text{Products}} \cdot \text{Differences}$$

$$\text{Tax (Local)}_{\text{Suppressed}} = \text{Tax (Local)}_{\text{Secondary}} + D_{\text{Local}} \cdot \text{Differences}$$

$$\text{Tax (State)}_{\text{Suppressed}} = \text{Tax (State)}_{\text{Secondary}} + D_{\text{State}} \cdot \text{Differences}$$

$$\text{Tax (Union)}_{\text{Suppressed}} = \text{Tax (Union)}_{\text{Secondary}} + D_{\text{Union}} \cdot \text{Differences}$$

Where: Differences are imponderable factors (active-1; inactive=0), that introduce values D_n in these equations making suppressed values different from secondary values.

These equations among other things, tell us the following:

A - Over all tax increase

If authorities suppress low tax paying markets for high tax paying markets they may increase over all taxation in the system, without using any appropriate laws for this objective. For instance, if informal markets, micro or small markets, low tech markets are substituted by consolidated or high-tech government secondary markets, then taxes will increase in the system.

B- Over all tax decrease

If the contrary occurs, then taxes will decrease in the environment. For instance, when authorities install a support system to deliver existential assistance to poor people funded with money collected from higher social classes, they collect less over all taxes after the system is in place, because they create a low margin secondary market in the process.

If this process continues to grow, tax collected must grow at a much faster pace than the assistance value being delivered; mainly if articulation also grows and reaches much higher levels. The same phenomenon occurs in any other subclasses.

These characteristics of support systems may be used as a powerful tool for restructuring the whole economic, political, social environment to benefit some classes and to harm other classes according to the will of those who control them.

03 Differentiation Market

When a social phenomenon - for instance a personal property - is registered in the democratic system its registered value is considered a "social – democratic" value. But all else, that is not registered by law - referring to that same phenomenon- may constitute social, natural, mental, or sovereign phenomenon. Notice that Objective Theory Study Areas reach only these phenomena as they relate to proper rule systems. Each one of them has its own specific social area of study; for instance sociology, political science economy etc…

Differentiation - is a difference among intrinsic and differentiated object price. **Intrinsic values** are prices in a perfect system. But as perfect systems do not exist in reality, than we use **more efficient real values** as a reference for **differentiation calculations**.

Differentiation Market is a mental place located in participants' minds, where differentiation values are established for the various services and goods in a specific society. They may represent gains or imposed losses for system agents according to their democratic situation. In this text we shall consider social-democratic differentiation markets; where differentiated prices are registered in proper rule system records. We call these records "Class Objects" of this market class.

3.1 - Class Analyses

The class equation for differentiated prices is as follows:

$$V_{Current} = V_{Intrinsic} + D.\,Will_{Social\,Demands}$$

Where: $V_{Current}$ is the differentiated price being paid in the market; $V_{Intrinsic}$ is the value for the same service, product or work being paid in a more efficient system; D is the differentiation being included in the equation by the imponderable factor. $Will_{Social\,Demands}$ is an imponderable factor (active=1; inactive=0) that introduces D into the equation.

As we see in this equation; differentiation exists because social agents who control their waves want them to exist. Whenever there is a differentiation process in the system, wave controllers become active and pass it on to other agents under their control. We have shown you the class analyses for this process in chapter "Class Limitations". And next chapter "Democracy Inefficiency" you will find the equilibrium equations that mathematically explain how this occurs. In this chapter we are interested in the social – democratic markets that are formed in these processes.

3.2 - Explanation Example

Let us consider that in a given day, a product constituted by the subclasses shown in the following figure 36 could be bought in a more efficient market place for 6 thousand dollars.

Each class contributed to a specific part worth 1 thousand dollars, at current prices. These specific objects will keep their structure, and we will let their prices fluctuate according to market place democratic conditions.

It also shows prices for those same parts but in another date in the same market place, and after a selective process was installed and produced differential effects.

Let us suppose that these numbers are the actual current prices for the same specific objects whose more efficient prices listed in the prior table. Also let us consider they represent only the effect of selective and systemic differentiation processes. The following table resumes the differentiation values for this explanation example:

These values are delivered together with work, goods or services, to market counterparts that receive them. As they may assume different prices according to market democratic conditions, they constitute a separate market in their own; that we call **Differentiation market.**

Example Class (Market Place)		
Subclass Object "More Efficient Product Value"		
Class	Value%	units
Work Pay	17%	1,000
Application Return	17%	1,000
Interest	17%	1,000
Goods	17%	1,000
Services	17%	1,000
Royalties	17%	1,000
" More Efficient Product Value"	**100%**	**6,000**
Subclass Object "Differentiated Product Value"		
Month	Value%	units
Work Pay	5%	300
Application Return	20%	1,200
Interest	22%	1,300
Goods	18%	1,100
Services	12%	700
Royalties	7%	400
"Differentiated Product Value"	**83%**	**5,000**
Subclass (Differentiation)		
Month	Value%	units
Work Pay	-12%	-700
Application Return	3%	200
Interest	5%	300
Goods	2%	100
Services	-5%	-300
Royalties	-10%	-600
Differentiation Object	**-17%**	**-1,000**

04 Differentiation Market Effect

Differentiation markets produce differences in the way people live socially, naturally, mentally and sovereignty, in different government systems across the world.

For instance a common worker in a more efficient system may have access to technological advanced products, but may not have access to housemaid service. Quite in the contrary a common worker in a deficient system may have access to housemaid service but not to technological advanced products.

By other side, affordability of high-tech products in more efficient systems, do not present significant social differential impact among people who live in more efficient systems; because most of the people may have access to them.

But in the opposite side, affordability of low paid services and products make a huge differential impact in social lives of people who live in deficient or inefficient systems, because they are affected by the differentiation market.

The following fictitious example show us the effect of differentiation processes in lives of employees, employers, poor medium and rich social classes.

4.1 - Medium Families Tax Disadvantage

The following figure 37 shows the effect of imbalanced taxes in the life of a Medium Lower Social Class (Family B), and Medium Higher Social Class (Family A):

In this table, we suppose that "Family A" earns 6 thousand dollars gross income; pays 2.5 thousand dollars in taxes; and gets back only 200 dollars in public services.

While "Family B" earns 3 thousand dollars gross income; pays 900 dollars in taxes; and gets back 750 dollars in public services.

As we can see, "Family A" and "Family B" without differentiation effect receive 3.7 and 2.85 thousand dollars net income respectively, in social-democratic revenue (that means social gain plus democratic gain).

Subclass Object "Family Income"

Aspects	Family A Value	Family B Value	Family A/B
Gross Income	6000	3000	200%
Tax Aliquot%	-42%	-30%	
Tax Value	-2500	-900	
Income After Taxes	3500	2100	
Public Service Received	200	750	
Net Income	3700	2850	130%
Imposed Loss	-2300	-150	
Imposed Loss%	-38%	-5%	

Subclass Object "Employee Income"

Aspects	Value	Family A/E	Family B/E
Gross Income	250	2300%	1100%
Tax aliquot%	0%		
Tax value	0		
Income After Taxes	250		
Public Service received	750		
Social - Democratic Income	1000	270%	200%
Democratic Gain	750		
Democratic gain%	300%		

Public Service Received

Class	Object
Scholl for two children	250
Family health plan	100
Retirement plan	25
Leisure programs	25
Subsidy in the form of cash	150
Residential subsidy	100
Other subsidy	100
Democratic – income	750

Notice that these numbers are only for illustrative purpose.

The effect of imbalanced taxes in medium family's budget is to destroy more, the higher social incomes, and destroy less the lower medium social incomes. This effect tends to level at some extent and by the lower side, the net income of medium families. In this case "Family A" received 200% of "Family B" gross income; but only 130% of net income. Because of it, gross income of different social classes may seem very different, but their net value, tend to approach the lower ones as aggressiveness heightens.

In this case Family A shows an imposed loss of 2.3 thousand dollars, and Family B shows an imposed loss of 150 dollars with this system. But all this, is without the effect of the Differentiation Market.

For those who believe the history ends here it is a bad business for medium families. But indeed the story does not end there; they just are not counting social compensation.

4.2 - Employee Democratic Advantage

Let us suppose that a housemaid employee has a social-democratic gain budget as shown in figure 37:

In this table we suppose employee income (housemaid) was 250 dollars as gross income; pays no taxes; and gets 750 dollars in public services for free. These services are explained in the following table in figure 37:

As we can see, these services constitute democratic gain for this class. That makes its net income go to 1 thousand dollars net in social democratic gain.

Notice that Family A earns 2.3 thousand per cent over this employee in gross terms. But when we consider the net income that advantage goes down to only 270 per cent. And Family B earns 1.1 thousand per cent over this employee in gross terms. But when we consider the net income that advantage goes down to only 200 per cent.

That looks like a great "miracle in the rules", and again for those who believe the story ends here it is a complete "success" in enriching the poor against the mediums. But indeed the story does not end there; they just are not counting social compensation.

4.3 - Employee Social Disadvantage

But that democratic disadvantage for the mediums activates them to exert their control over labor relation to demand social compensation from the employee. The result of their demand is reflected already in labor price. The following figure 38 shows how this effect is occurring.

We suppose in this table that the real intrinsic value of the work done by a housemaid service is 2,500 dollars in a more efficient real system. As the current salary paid is just 250 dollars than the employer is earning 2,250 dollars back right from the employee. That is a compensation payment that the employee is paying to the employer for government system deficiencies.

As we also see in that table this housemaid earns 750 dollars in free public services, that indeed just pays back to her some of the compensation paid. But she still loses a **difference** of 1.5 thousand dollars due to system aggressive activity and social compensation. It is equivalent to a **social tribute** at the rate of 60% over her gross intrinsic income.

If we factor in the interest rates, of just 12% a year, monthly capitalized, than along her entire career as a poor employee, she will deliver millions of dollars' worth in compensation to her employers.

"Employee Compensation Market"

Aspects	Value
Intrinsic Salary Value	2500
Current Salary Value	250
Compensation to Employer	-2250
Public Service received "Free"	750
Compensated Loss	-1500
Compensated Loss%	-60%

"Employer Compensation Market"

Employee	Compensation
1	2250
2	4500
3	6750
4	9000

4.4 - Employer Social Advantage

That allows us to measure the differentiation market impact in social lives of "Family A" and "Family B" according to the following tables. Fist let us show the compensation prices in the Differentiation Market. That is also shown in figure 38.

As we see 1 employee gives 2.25 thousand dollars in compensation, 2 employees 4.5 thousand dollars and so forth.

The impact of this market in the lives of employers depends on their individual attributes and life style. In our case, we have a family that employs housemaid. Than it depends on their net income and on the number of housemaids the family employs. The next tables in figure 39 explain this for "Family A" and "Family B".

Differentiation Market Effect: Family A				
	Employee	Income	Compensated Gain	Compensated Gain%
Gross Income		6.000	0	0%
Net Income		3.700	-2.300	-38%
Compensated Income	1	5.950	-50	-1%
Compensated Income	2	8.200	2.200	37%
Compensated Income	3	10.450	4.450	74%
Compensated Income	4	12.700	6.700	112%
Differentiation Market Effect: Family B				
	Employee	Income	Compensated Gain	Compensated Gain%
Gross Income		3.000	0	0%
Net Income		2.850	-150	-5%
Compensated Income	1	5.100	2.100	70%
Compensated Income	2	7.350	4.350	145%
Compensated Income	3	9.600	6.600	220%
Compensated Income	4	11.850	8.850	295%

As we see, with one employee "Family A" is losing only -1% with this system. And with 2 employees "Family A" is gaining a 37% increase in its gross income with the presence of this system. But still there are to be counted plenty of other gains such as lower prices in restaurants, hotels, schools, and all other services.

As we see, with one employee "Family B" is gaining 70% with this system. And with 2 employees "Family B" is gaining a 145% increase in its gross income with the presence of this system. And also there are to be counted plenty of other gains.

That means considering a family with 2 housemaids; a 3 thousand dollars gross income in a deficient system provides a social democratic net income that is worth more than 5.1 thousand dollars plus taxes in a more efficient system. Considering a 30% tax in the more efficient system then a family needs 7.3 thousand dollars in gross income to be able to hire two housemaids.

In other words, 3 thousand dollars in a deficient system buys the same social status as 7.3 thousand dollars in a more efficient system. In this case we consider 2 housemaids as a social status.

This is precisely why medium families as a general rule, do not seem to bother at all with politics in deficient systems. And because of this apathy, they end up offering few or none, resistance, to eventual creation of more reaching and more aggressive support systems until their social advantage is really in clear jeopardy by some of them.

The advantages are higher for lower medium class families who can use housemaids, or other employees; be it in their homes or in their personal businesses. Those who chose to, or simply cannot use employees, are not able to collect this direct benefit from deficient systems.

Yet everybody that lives in deficient systems may benefit from lower prices for goods and services offered; some even in the piracy market. But most of those who do not live on capital gains have to pay compensation in their pay checks, and face violence and other disadvantages in different degrees according to their personal life style.

CHAPTER 15

DEMOCRACY INEFFICIENCY

Interactive Class Effects – constitute "real class objects" of interactive waves that may be observed in day to day reality, most of the time as disconnected phenomenons. In the prior chapter we considered interactive waves and correspondent interactive class effects of; Secondary Assistance; and Differentiation Market. In this chapter we shall discuss Democracy Inefficiency. And in the next chapter we shall discuss Qualitativity.

01 Democracy Inefficiency

Democracy Inefficiency is an imposed loss on participants by any of the existential environments, due to inappropriate consequent behavior of democracy. We also may call democracy inefficiency as market inefficiency.

It is different from state inefficiency and system inefficiency but these are keyphenomenato its existence. And it may present itself in many different ways, but at the end of the day, all of them meaning the very same thing to system participants; **imposed loss**.

We may classify **democracy inefficiency** according to the source, or the environment, that is originating the imposed loss to participants. In this text we shall consider Systemic Inefficiency, Social Inefficiency, and Quality Inefficiency.

02 Democracy Systemic Inefficiency

2.1 - State Inefficiency

You probably have already heard about state inefficiency or state deficiency, which may be defined as an imposed loss against participants derived from the actions of state officials. However, state officials do not actuate at once, in all aspects of any proper rule environment. Rather they selectively chose aspects and objectives, define strategies and act accordingly, in due time. When they do just that, they may be inefficient and may impose a loss on democracy. This works as a selective differentiation process that in its turn activates systemic differentiation processes that affect all aspects of the democratic environment as a consequence. That is one of the reasons why democratic markets increase or decrease differentiation presence on its price as a whole.

2.2 - System Intrinsic Inefficiency

But let us suppose that state officials stop producing inefficiency at certain time; and do their work efficiently thereon. In that case the existing system differential differences would not simply go away; they would initially stay exactly where they were.

This means **system differentiation** present in a system at a given time is not a direct consequence of state inefficiency. Rather it is a consequence of accumulated past government inefficiencies. They constitute what we call **system intrinsic inefficiency**.

System Intrinsic inefficiency, are imposed losses on a real democracy in comparison with a perfect system. The following figure explains this thought.

HOW TO THINK AND REALIZE OBJECTIVES UNDER ANY PROPER RULE ENVIRONMENT

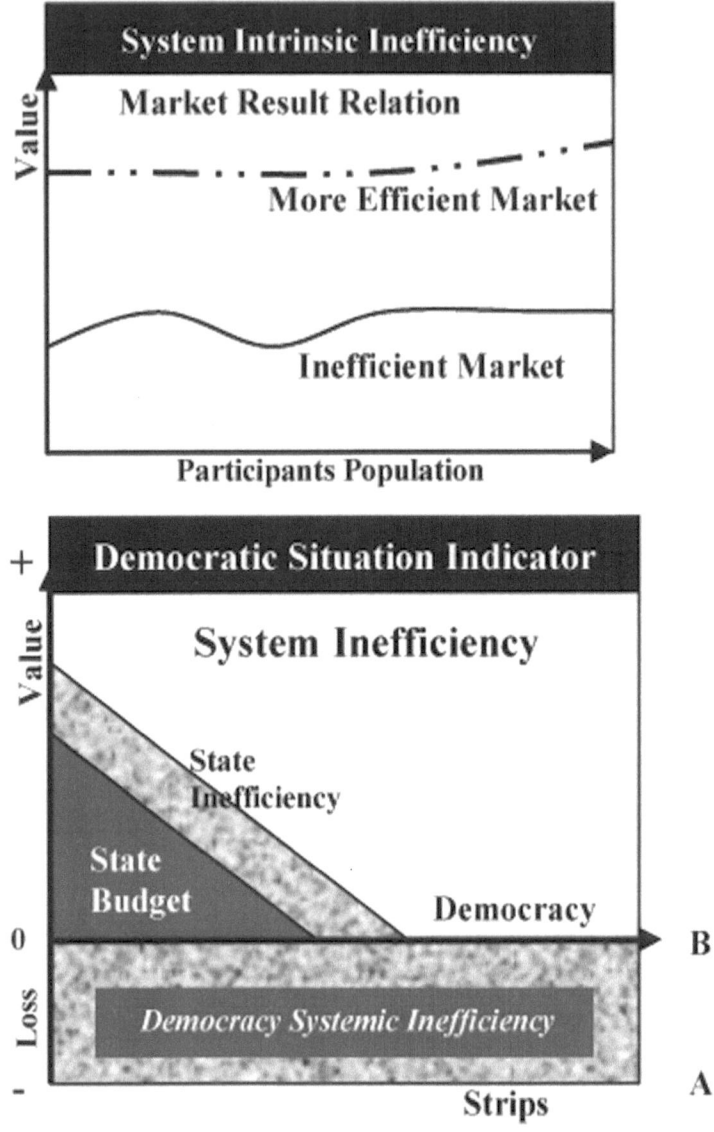

This figure illustrates that more efficient systems exhibit a market result relation with participant's population that is higher than inefficient systems. The difference is system intrinsic inefficiency. **System intrinsic inefficiency** is responsible for the cost of transforming existential resources into useful goods and services by and within, one proper rule system that is serving a society.

2.3 - Democracy Systemic Inefficiency

By other side, we may say that, at a given time, an inefficient government is adding to the system its own dose of differential differences. To that we call Market Systemic Inefficiency, or Democracy Systemic Inefficiency.

Democracy Systemic Inefficiency is an imposed loss on democracy derived from present government inefficiencies. Together Democracy and State Inefficiency constitute System Inefficiency. The following figure illustrates this concept:

This is a **Democratic Situation Indicator** where democracy is represented by strips of participant situations ordered by value and piled up one on top of the other. We also find in this figure the government which is represented in **allocation method** of aspects; people and value. Inefficiency appears as an extra strip in the button of democracy, and also as a strip that reduces state disposable budget. Inefficiency means budget loss for government and situation loss for participants. That means many people could be better off; but they are not; in face of inefficiency that is eating up their returns, and not letting them accumulate as attributes.

03 How to reduce Democracy Systemic Inefficiency

Inefficiency is a cost formed by values that are lost by classes of participants, due to the existence of undesired occurrences. Also according to the Objective Theory, it is an exclusive characteristic of autocratic mode operating systems. That means democratic or autocratic system when they operate in democratic mode conceptually, they do not produce inefficiency.

Therefore we may reduce democracy systemic inefficiency simply by increasing the relative presence of democratic mode operating systems in the whole considered system.

We may do that by the side of government with government side reforms, and also by the side of democracy by reducing specific democracy inefficiencies.

In this chapter we shall discuss by the government side; **Government Size**, and **Government Quality** Reforms.

And also in this chapter we shall discuss by the democracy side; **Social Inefficiency** and **Quality Inefficiency**.

In the next chapter we shall discuss **Qualitativity Inefficiency.**

3.1- Adjust Government Size (State/System Relation)

Government systems are composed of autocratic and democratic systems, which operate in democratic or autocratic mode. The Objective theory accepts that democratic principles constitute a perfect democratic system; which is the most efficient system possible.

Because of that we say that relation between democratic over autocratic operating mode shall define government inefficiency and consequently democratic systemic inefficiency. We call this relation Government Quality.

Government Quality is the relation between democratic over autocratic operating mode systems within a state.

If we change the size, of a particular government, in relation to the whole proper rule system, than the government quality – or operating mode relation - naturally changes and the consequent democracy inefficiency, also changes. The following figures illustrate the effect of government growth in size with relation to a system size.

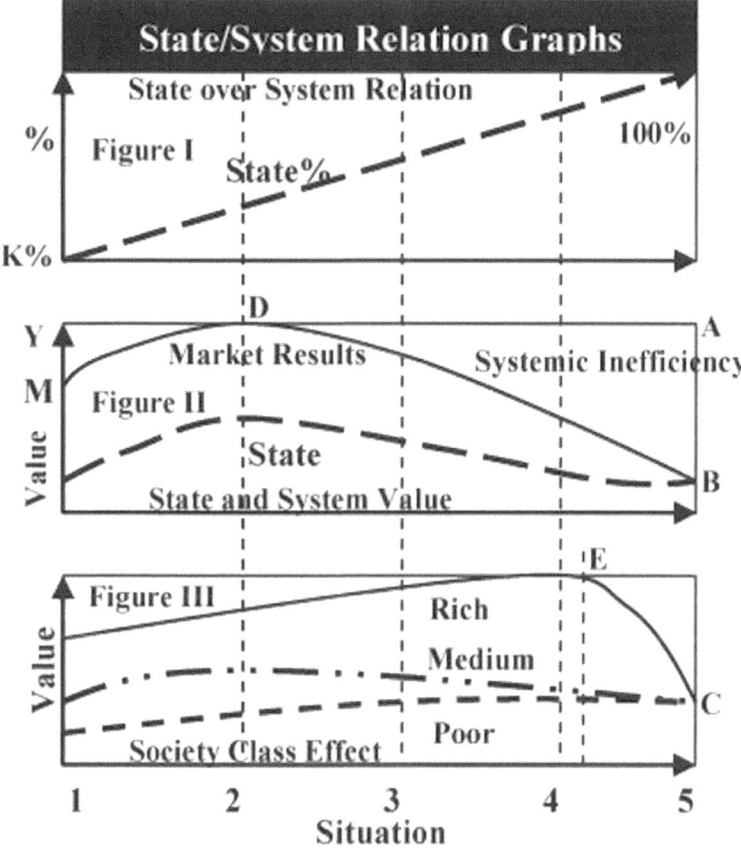

Figure I - shows Percent State/System Relation that is changing from K% to 100%

Figure II - shows Market Result value and State value; that change as an exclusive consequence of State/System Relation variation. The area between line YDA and curve MDB is democracy systemic inefficiency.

Figure III - shows: Rich, Medium and Poor Classes Situation Values.

Situations 1 to 5 and E, in different state/system relation, are common to all figures. These numbers where put in these figures taking into consideration the natural order of things. Just to make possible the explanation, about what is it that conceptually happens to them, in case the percent state/system relation grows until 100%. In these figures all else is considered invariable except the State/System Relation and its consequences on the aspects analyzed.

More Efficient Relation Zone - We observe that if government grows in situations 1 until situation 2, market results also grow simply by that (notice that conceptually in this case there is no other circumstance involved). At the same time, situation value of rich, medium and poor classes of participants; also grow.

We call any of these situations efficient state/relation situations, and they all altogether by More Efficient Relation Zone.

Inefficient Relation Zone - We also observe that if government continues to grow after situation 2, until situation 5, than Market Results fall exclusively because of that. That is; Market Results fall because of the weight of the State.

We call any of these situations inefficient state/relation situations, and they all altogether by Inefficient Relation Zone

Notice that between situation 1 and 2 system inefficiency was reducing. But it starts to increase after situation 2 and finishes with maximum value AB in situation 5. That is called **maximum inefficiency state/system relation.**

We also observe that **rich class situation value** may continue to grow after situation 2, until situation E that is after situation 4. After that, **rich situation value** falls very sharply until situation 5 (may be as a result of some violent movement). Because of that conceptual circumstance, situation E is called **Break Point** of State/System Relation.

The **medium class situation value** starts to fall in situation 2, and continues to fall until situation 5.

The **poor class situation value** meanwhile, goes up until situation 5; that is not very far upward from their initial situation.

Therefore we may say that; rich and poor classes of participants may profit inefficient systems, while medium class pay imposed losses.

That is exactly why there is a constant pressure for inefficient democratic systems with a vast population of poor people, to operate with inefficient state system relations. Consequently, adding yet more differential differences to their systems.

The reason for the profit to rich class is capital value; that goes up in inefficient systems. And the reason for poor class profit is subsidy; that also goes up in inefficient systems.

To reduce inefficiency - we should increase the size of government in more efficient relation zone. Or reduce the size of a government in inefficient relation zone.

3.2 - Improve Government Quality
(Democratic/Autocratic Operating Mode Relation)

Intrinsic Government Quality is the democratic/ autocratic operating mode relation that does not present any Democracy Systemic Inefficiency. It corresponds to situation D in Figure B; which one corresponds to situation 2.

If participants want to continue in a more efficient relation zone and also to grow government participation in the system, than they must precede some government democratic reform, which conceptually put the Intrinsic Government Quality forward in the graph. In other words; the more democratic systems are present in a State, the higher Intrinsic Government Quality is.

But if in the contrary to this, some autocratic reforms are put into the system, then the Intrinsic Government Quality moves backward making more efficient systems less efficient or even inefficient; and inefficient systems more inefficient.

04 Democracy Social Inefficiency

4.1 – Government/Democracy Quality Relation

Evidently State and Democracy are very different environments. Democracy is a collection of people who can vote in a proper rule system, and may use their freedom to actuate as social, natural, mental, and sovereign agents. In other words, people who participate in a democracy normally do many things not related to the system at all. Whereas state officials worry about well being of all people; democracy agents most of the time, worry about their own well being. They pursue profit; that is nothing short of favorable imbalances. In other words; while state is trying to balance things up, democracy is naturally trying to gain more profit; one agent against others. States main rule in Democracy is Regulation in order to limit markets agents' power. But government cannot control democratic agents themselves. The following figure 42 illustrates these thoughts.

Figure's 38 upper part is a democratic situation indicator for a certain market service showing ordered and, one on top of the other, strips of service value in a considered aspect. Democracy and State are separately plotted to show you their differences. Regulation takes all state classes while in the market place it appears separated in the button as a "no go zone" strip; indicating no one could go below it.

But regulation does not reach the infinite aspects of reality; only some key aspects of reality are limited by government through regulation. All other infinite aspects concerning exactly the same services or products are not regulated by government. Supposedly they are regulated by society itself, through market negotiation, which is a social activity. We could even say that "they are controlled by the invisible hand of society" - which in our class math, it means; the imponderable factor of "society will". Figure's 42 lower part "Fictitious Service Industry" illustrates this thought.

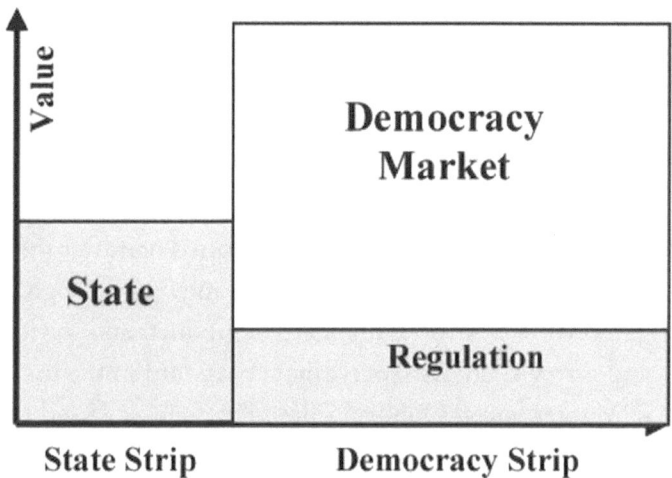

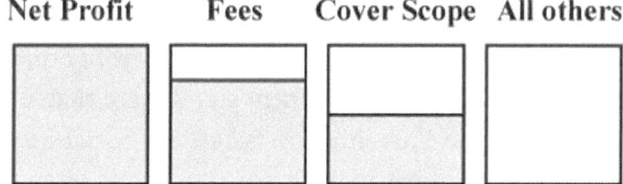

These figures show regulation in some aspects of a fictitious service industry and the all others aspects that are not regulated. In all, or some of these infinite others aspects market agents may adjust their industry to any pressure that may come from government, society or even nature.

4.2 – Democracy Social More Efficiency

Conceptually a democratic system may not hurt any one of its participants. Because of this characteristics authorities' mission, when regulating a market is to avoid any kind of **Democracy Systemic Inefficiency**. For this to happen, they establish and enforce some **important existential standards** - in natural, social, mental and sovereign environments. We call these regulation requirements **Government Enforced Quality.**

By other side, because of society rule in the market, it also forms its own market existential standards. We call these market common practices or **Market Social Quality**. The following figure's 43 upper part, shows these concepts.

This figure is a Democratic Situation Indicator Way; it shows profiles of various democratic situation indicators plotted one after the other, as time goes on. It shows the way situations are moving through out time. In this figure, Arrow S is Social Standard of products and services sold or bought; and arrow G shows Government Standard in the market. The line M_Q - "Market Social Quality" - describes values offered in services and products in this market. The line G_Q - "Government Enforced Quality" - describes the minimum existential standards accepted in this market. Notice that government is imposing on real markets, democratic or autocratic principles, to limit market social quality. That means regulation describes literally what these considered minimum existential standards, are. In these conditions S, is greater than G; telling us that, it is possible to raise government standard to that level without disturbing this market. This situation is called a Social More efficient Democracy or Market. That is:

Democracy Social More Efficiency is a Government/ Democracy Quality Relation where Social Market Quality is above Government Enforced Quality.

4.3 – Social Quality Differentiation

Social Quality Differentiation is a difference in quality introduced in a product or service by a social agent. Normally, in a social quality differentiation event, the social agent changes the quality of his or her own products, or services, that are being offered in the market.

Any social agent may offer a product, or service, that is quality differentiated with relation to the ones currently offered in the market. If the quality differentiation is for a higher quality, than we call it **qualification**. If it is for a lower quality, than we call it **disqualification**.

Quality differentiation occurs in services or products; in other words, it occurs in agent's attributes not on agents them selves.

When social agents offer services that are better quality differentiated; naturally they elevate the market social quality. And if too many other agents also actuate in the same way, that becomes a common behavior in that society. So, social market quality will go up wile this trend continues.

4.4 – Democracy Social Inefficiency

By the other side, when social agents offer a lesser quality differentiated service, they lower the social market quality. And if too many of them follow through this path, than market social quality may fall even below government enforced quality. This situation we call democracy social inefficiency.

Notice that, social disqualification may come after a natural, social or rule unrest. For instance, after a government has disqualified some regulation for a market. Or after any unrest in world market as a whole has occurred. Or even after any important natural phenomenon that permanently affect social life.

Democracy Social Inefficiency - is a situation where market social quality fall below government enforced quality. The following figure's 43 middle part, illustrates this concept.

In this figure, after time 3, **democracy is socially inefficient**. Because not accepted social practices are occurring on it. In a situation of social inefficiency the system is not able to attend something that is officially expected from it. For instance a minimum wage that is not being paid in full extent; this difference is social inefficiency of democracy.

If for whatever reason, disposable value is temporarily reduced in an environment, than many people are forced to reduce the quality of their work, products or services just to copy with the market lowering trend; all that is social inefficiency.

05 How to reduce Democracy Social Inefficiency

Democracy Social Inefficiency is a democratic phenomenon that occurs because of social agents actions. That means we cannot counter it simply by government reforms. A government controls its own environment but do not control democracy agents. Democratic agents are free to actuate also as any other environment agents. Government does not control nature, than good sense is necessary to understand what can and cannot be naturally changed. Government does not control society, than persuasion is necessary to lure social agents for contributing to a social efficiency project. Government does not control thoughts and decisions of mental and sovereign agents, than information and elections are need to obtain their accordance. As we may see neither any general, nor any hero is required for this, because it is not a one man mission. It is a very difficult and costly constructive process that indeed requires no less than a democratic "leader of the masses" to accomplish this mission.

06 Democracy Quality Inefficiency

6.1 – Government Quality Differentiation

Authorities also perform quality differentiation. For instance, they may increase government enforced quality to incorporate some of the democracy social more efficiency quality. Further ahead in time, they may repeat that process to accommodate more of it; and so forth. When they do this they are quality differentiating the market. In this case they are qualifying it.

But let us suppose that when facing a social inefficiency situation, authorities are unable or unwilling to enforce existing law to make social agents comply with. Instead they reform legislation and reduce the minimum existential standards that, they themselves, have to enforce. By doing this they are quality differentiating the market also. In this case they are disqualifying it.

Notice that in a selective differentiation process, authorities are actuating directly upon democracy, forcing classes of agents to do or not do something. That is; they actuate forcefully upon people. Differently in the case of quality differentiation, authorities simply allow people to behave in certain conditions. They actuate upon services and products, that is; they actuate upon agents attributes.

6.2- Democracy Quality Inefficiency

Let us suppose that, for whatever reason, a social market quality that is being practiced in a market is imposing losses to some participant classes in a proper rule system.

Conceptually the democratic system objective is the well being of all participants. From this principle comes the concept for quality inefficiency.

Democracy Quality Inefficiency is a situation where government enforced market quality is causing the presence of democracy inefficiency. That means it is causing systemic losses to some participant classes to occur in the democratic environment.

It may occur by insufficient information about product, service or work characteristics. It may come as a function of unforeseen changes that may occur in the existential environment. Or, it may come for any other cause; including a government disqualification process to abide social inefficiency.

For instance let us consider that there is a social inefficiency in a certain market. And because of it, government lowers the enforced market quality to make that social inefficiency legal.

But the lower social market quality may impose more losses to participant classes, that simply where unknown of before.

Or it may be that, the democracy quality inefficiency was already seen by government officials, and just has increased as a function of the disqualification process. The following figure's 43 lower part, illustrates this concept.

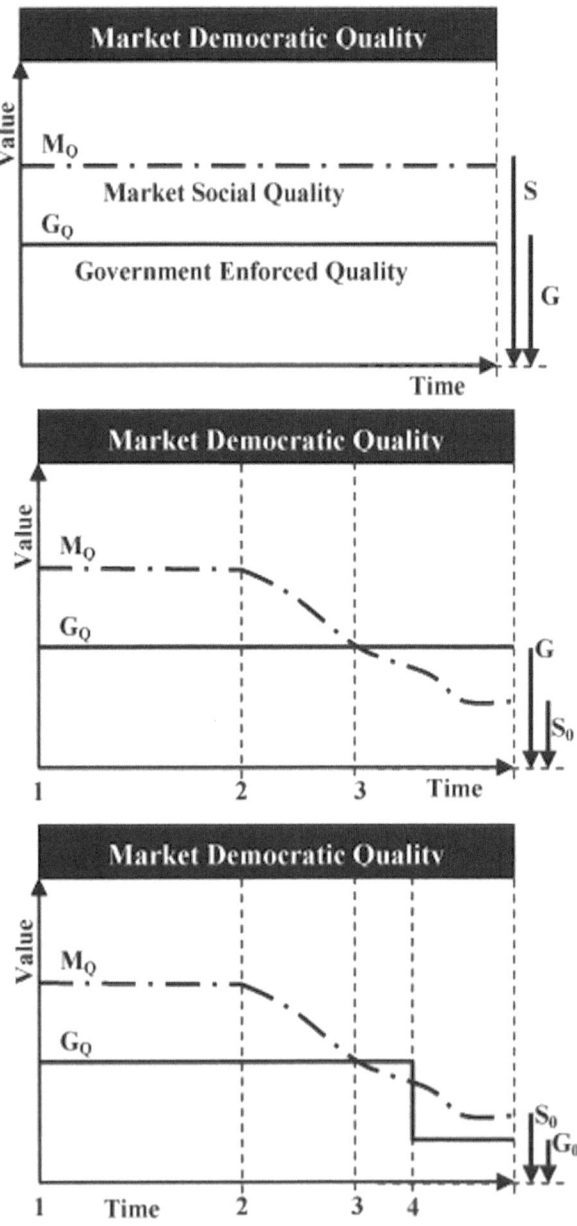

In time 4 authorities put into activity a law that requires lower existential standards. Literally they brought into the system, all social inefficiency that existed in society, making it, or increasing its existing quality inefficiency.

6.3 - Democracy Quality Class Equation

There is a class equation that explains quality Differentiation as follows:

$$D_0 = D - D_1 \cdot \text{Will}_{\text{Authorities}}$$

Where: D is the prior minimum existing existential standards; D_0 is the actual existential standard required; D_1 is an objective value subtracted from D, that is introduced by the imponderable factor; and $\text{Will}_{\text{Authorities}}$ is the imponderable factor that when active introduces D_1 into the equation (Active=1; Inactive=0).

07 Democracy Quality Inefficiency Effects

Social disqualification effects, may present themselves in any social aspect. In this chapter we shall discuss its effect on economics, politics and people's lives. To better understand the consequences of disqualification let us consider the following examples A and B:

7.1 - Examples

Example A- Let us suppose that a certain physician is attending 100 clients every month; at an individual price of 200 monetary units; and he spends 60 minutes with each client. To receive his clients, accommodate, and drive them to his attending place; he pays a secretary a fixed salary of 1 thousand monetary units; and also he pays other costs of 4 thousand monetary units each month. So, this physician receives net for his activities 15 thousand monetary units each month.

7.2 - Disqualification example A

Let us suppose that for whatever reason, this physician decides to attend his clients in 15 minutes. That is a **disqualification** of his work in the aspect "time spent with the client". Let us suppose demand fills all the exceeding time with new clients. And now he attends 4 clients in one hour instead of one client. That means he attends 400 clients every month and earns a gross value of 80 thousand monetary units every month. Now let us say he pays 2 thousand to 2 secretaries that attend 2 clients each. And let us say he pays 6 thousand for other costs. All that; lets him with 72 thousand monetary units net each month. For this physician **disqualification** mint a 260% income hike. For the workers it mint 1 working place, and double the work to do.

Example B - Let us suppose that in a certain society one person has to study 11 years to qualify for a university course and then be able to obtain his graduation degree. Normally people starts to study at 7 years old, and finishes basic education at 18 years old when he is able to enter university. Also normally, let's say H thousand people graduate each year in a number N of universities. Let us consider this is a deficient democratic system, and so being, only 10% of its 18 year old people, complete basic education. Thus, 90% of 18 years old boys and girls are not qualified for university courses. Because of this social inefficiency; there is already, in the system a way to shortcut such education requirement, by doing an official supplementary test at age 30 or above. This test substitutes all the 11 years of education; but the required high age, makes it impossible for the approved to compete with those who complete his basic education normally.

7.3 - Disqualification example B

Let us suppose that political authorities decide to disqualify the education system in order to provide access to universities to people without sufficient or adequate study. Let us say political authorities reduce the age required for government supplementary test to only 18 years old. Now; those even with no prior education at all, once approved in such simple tests, are ready to compete for university places with those who studied 11 years.

To make accessibility yet more inclusive let's say political authorities create heavy quotas exclusively reserved to those who complete basic education in public schools. And they decide to donate or subsidize money to those who have no monetary conditions to pay university tuitions. Also political authorities reduce standards, and also make a blind eye to all **disqualification,** universities themselves can put into their services. Universities lower as much as they can, the quality of the courses they offer in order to reduce prices of their tuitions. Such low prices allow these same political authorities to put more subsidized people in them; all paid by public money.

The results of all such **disqualification** processes are certainly astounding:

- a- University accessibility may explode to reach half or more of the 18 years old population, in that society.

- b- Numbers of places in the universities must grow to a much larger number to accommodate these people. And new universities need to be created literally everywhere.

- c- After some years X times H thousand people graduate each year in a number Y times N of universities.

- d- But the number of jobs may not have grown even a small fraction of that X. Notice that authorities do not create value, they simply protect value or officially change their owner, and nothing more. And university places keep sending graduates to the market years and years without stop.

- e- Thus **social inefficiency** grows to record numbers; most of these freshman graduates are working in other professions where their titles were not required before, or that even are not required at all, or simply they are not working. Also the pressure of a much higher number of graduates, seeking jobs makes the whole class salaries fall heavily, and they stabilize in unprecedented low levels.

f- Also **quality inefficiency** burst to a level never seen before: All doctors, businessmen, service man, and any other person who are able to, they do engage in some kind of **disqualification** to protect their social standards of living, or simply to **enrich** in the process.

08 Disqualification Result

Disqualification Result is any additional result produced by a disqualification process. It may represent gain to someone and imposed loss to others. As we have seen in the examples, disqualification losses occur in aspects relative to people's lives, while disqualification gains occur in economics related aspects.

In resume for those who could benefit **disqualification** – mainly the socially more strong agents - it mint profit growth; for all others – the vast majority of affected people - it mint salary reduction, time and resources lost, low paying and low qualified jobs.

Notice that in example A even if that physician decided to cut price of his service in a way that he would not have any economic benefit from disqualification, the overall economy would benefit from the increased movement that the lowering of price for a consultation would bring any way.

09 Gain for investors

Let us consider the same state/system relation graph seen in section "Government Size". Let us suppose that politician authorities want to make government size grow and put into place some, as they call them;

"inclusive measures". These are indeed disqualification processes much like the ones we studied in example B.

The following figure illustrates these consequences for variation K% until K_1% in State/ System Relation:

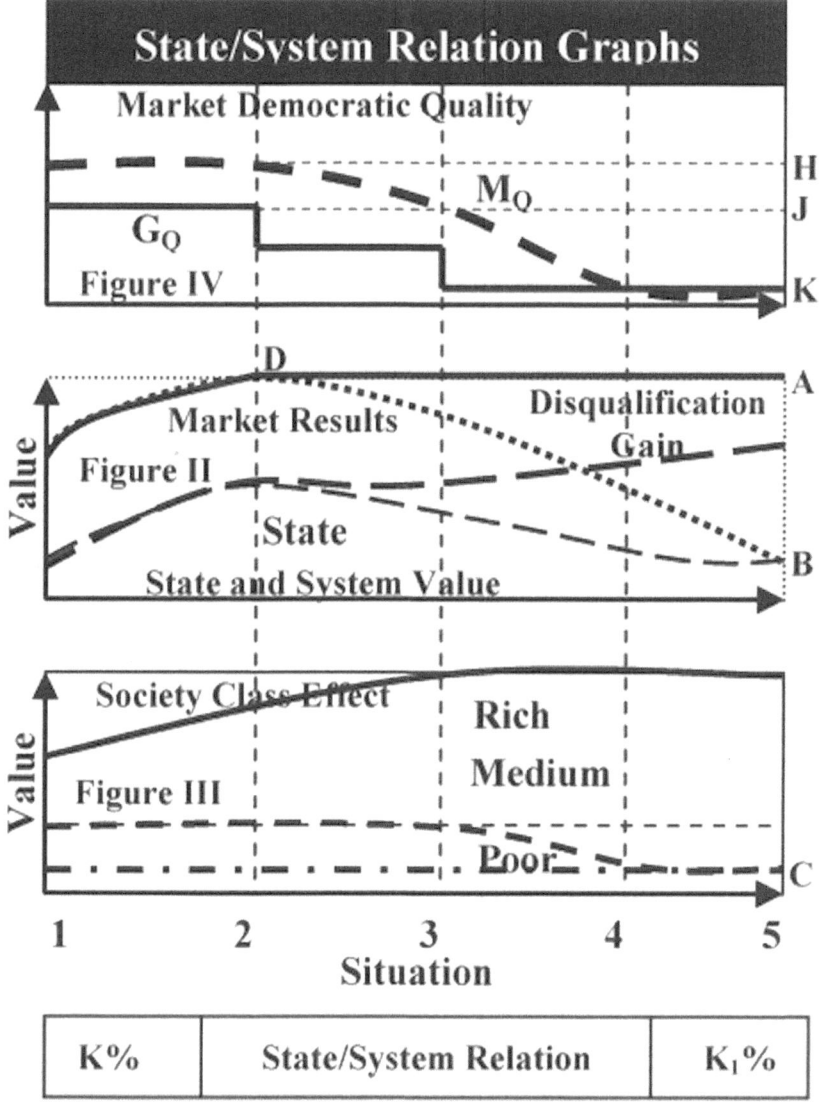

Figure IV – Shows that "Market Social Quality" (M_Q) and "Government Enforced Quality" (G_Q) started to fall in situation 2; taking the overall market, to a Quality Inefficient Market after situation 3 figure III; where medium class agent's situation start and continued to lose value until situation 5.

Figure II - shows Market Result value and State value; that change as exclusive consequence of two phenomena; Growth in State/System Relation and Disqualification.

In this case disqualification gain is supplying all the necessary income to counter the losses that could come as a result of State/ System Relation Growth. That means as State grows its relative size until K_1%, it is also made less and less qualified.

Figure III - shows: Rich, Medium and Poor Classes Situation Values.

Class (Rich) maintains its prosperity level without any risk while the disqualification process goes on. Class (Medium), stays leveled until situation 3 then it descends in search of Class (Poor) level. And Class (Poor) may have some small gains while the disqualification process goes on.

10 Advantage for Political Authorities

To understand the political advantage stemming from disqualification let us compare attributes of class (electoral power) with class (social income power). That is power of vote versus power of money income. To do so let us consider that we have a democratic community with only 10 participants.

Now let us ordinate them by income value – notice that "value" means action power in the democratic game. Than we are able to draw their income profile as seen in the following figure's 45 upper part.

This profile shows the income of each agent in a fictitious unity, side by side, in our fictitious community, ordered from higher to lower. And they are classified in four classes A to D according to their income. And these classes are ordered from higher to lower. We may profile any attribute that we wish in our fictitious community. Let us now profile the voting power: as shown in the following figure.

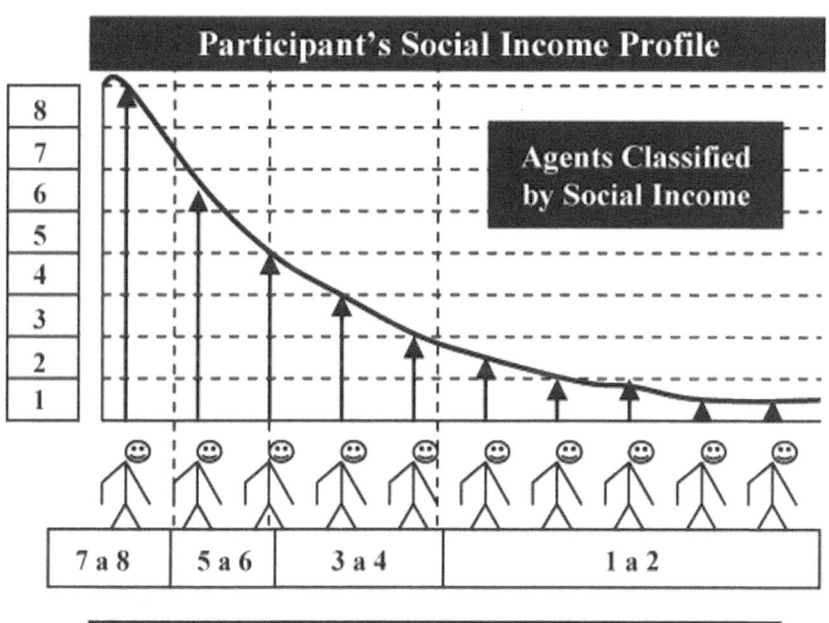

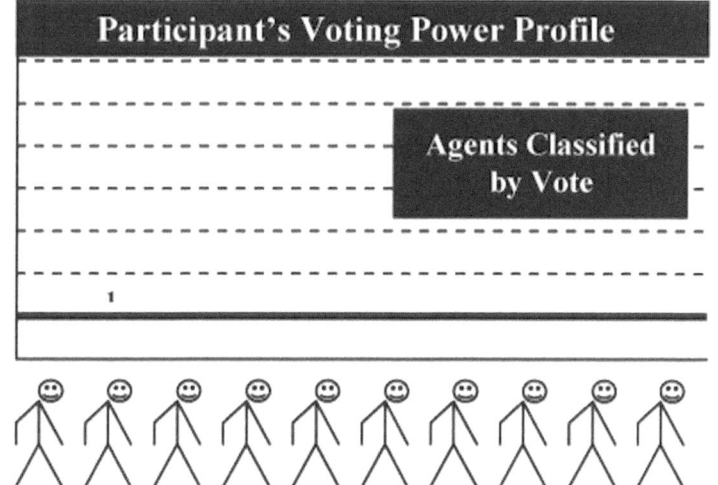

This profile shows that each participant is entitled to one single vote. At first glance this looks quite inoffensive. But when we apply the voting power to the income classes everything changes. As seen in the following figure's 46 upper part.

This is an illustration of a **comparison indicator**. In the line below we find all participants distributed within their income classes – from lower to higher. On the right side of the indicator we find the scale for income power that guides the income power line profile – a continuous line labeled "Income Power". On the left side of the figure we find the scale for the number of votes that exists in each participant class – segmented line labeled "Voting Power".

When we analyze these data we find that those with the least income – class D – almost can control the whole system themselves alone. Because, they have 5 votes out of 10 that exists in the whole community. To control the system and impose their will against all other's interests, they need just to do some kind of agreement with someone in a higher class - and they may prefer to favor the rich, through someone who represent them. We call this agreement Weak and Strong Agreement. These arrangements may include give away benefits for their class, and other benefits such as inclusion directly in other more sophisticated social classes, **exactly, through disqualification.**

So, when politician **authorities disqualify** a system regulation; they **may ear as many votes** as the number of persons direct benefited with the **giveaway.**

11 Imposed Loss on people's lives

The combined effects of disqualification mean increased net income for those who live on application returns. But at the same time, it means, more work, for less salary to those who live on work.

Social inefficiency makes it much harder to get a better return for a work done. For instance one may go to college but after this, he may not get a job in the profession he studied. That means this person end up working in another less qualified profession for a lower pay. This difference is formed exactly by **social inefficiency cost**.

Social inefficiency cost is all that is lost because of social inefficiencies. **Social inefficiency cost** is a social but personal cost that has to be paid by the social agent himself; and it does not count for over all economics result. Because of these characteristics it may grow to a very high number in the system without being ever noticed by any one. And still people may be willing to make it higher, because **disqualification** may be pleasing application holders and politicians. The following figure's 46 lower part, illustrates this concept.

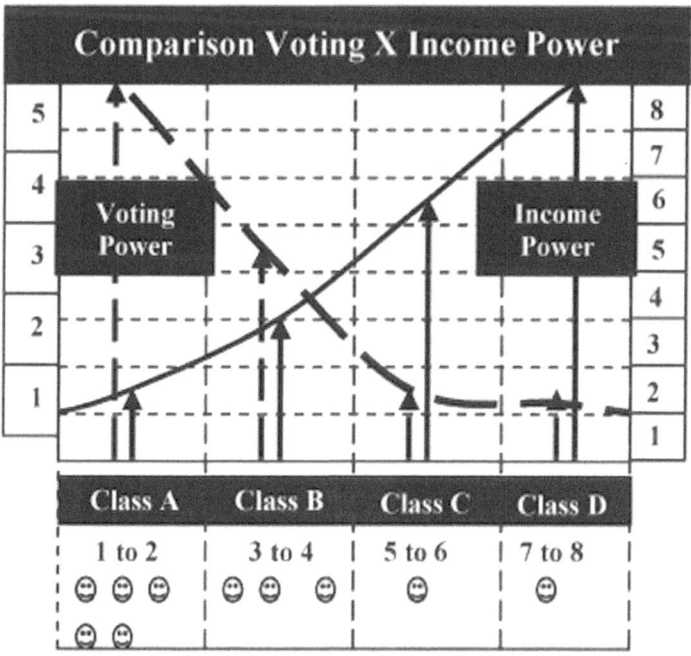

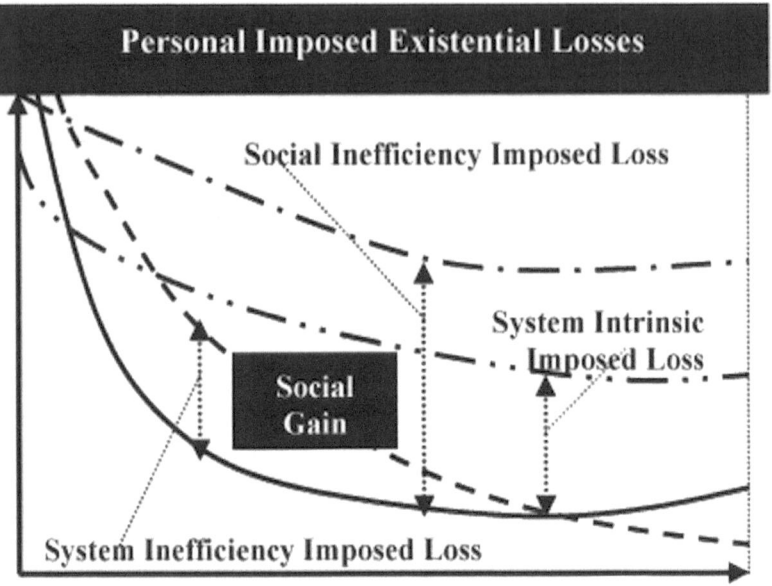

12 The Bubble Effect

A **Market Bubble** is a situation where relations involving one certain set of aspects get out of their normal behavior due to disqualification of the market they are traded in. Take for instance the two bubble events cited below where disqualification may cause serious imposed losses to people.

12.1 - Education Bubble

It occurs when educated people far exceed market needs. They are formed by disqualification of education industry and its accessibility.

For instance, let us say a government official wants to educate in superior level most of the poor people in society. The easiest way to do this is trough an education disqualification process. Let us say that currently it is necessary 11 years of prior minor level education to qualify; than this authority puts this requirement down by demanding only a simple set of tests that are applied in just one week. Also currently it is very expansive to study in superior level; than this authority decides to pay for all those who wants to study and demands no pay back for that. For this he creates all sorts of incentives, and in addition to that he also demand universities to lower the quality of their classes including using no books, less qualified teachers, and shortening the duration of their curses. Yes, in example B we have an education bubble! The following figure's 47 upper part illustrates an education bubble event.

On stack A we have a situation without education bubble. And on stack B we have an education bubble. Social classes are classified by the LIRA Method as follows: Class (Rich) or Class (1) - are those who live on capital investments; Class (Medium) or Class (2) - are those who live on work. They may be capital investors or superior educated workers. Class (Poor) or Class (3) - are those who live on personal government subsidy in any extent.

The effect of increased superior education range on the democratic environment is the impoverishment of the majority in medium Class (2), who are superior educated workers. All happens like this: a- Class (3) increases offer on superior educated workers; b- than wages go down; c- and most superior educated workers also go to Class (3).

Notice that Class (3) in undeveloped world grows at a much higher pace than Class (2). That means the impoverishment process of educated workers has no limits; and may even go to zero for many people. By other side people that can no longer leave the slums by means of education may resort to violence to change the system trough sophisticated urban war.

12.2 - Stock Prices Bubble

It occurs when prices far exceed substantial price. They are formed by disqualification in prices of goods, services or rights. When prices are going higher without substantial value increase, there is no problem; everybody is happy. But when the bubble bursts there are imposed losses everywhere. The following figure's 47 lower part, illustrates this thought.

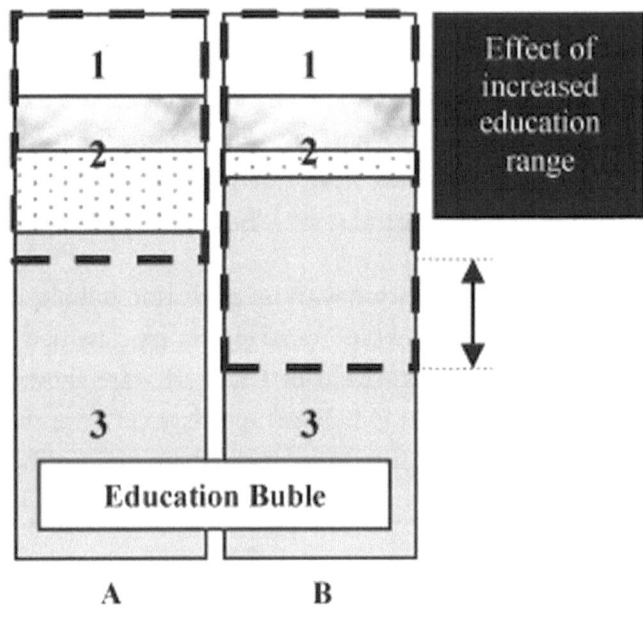

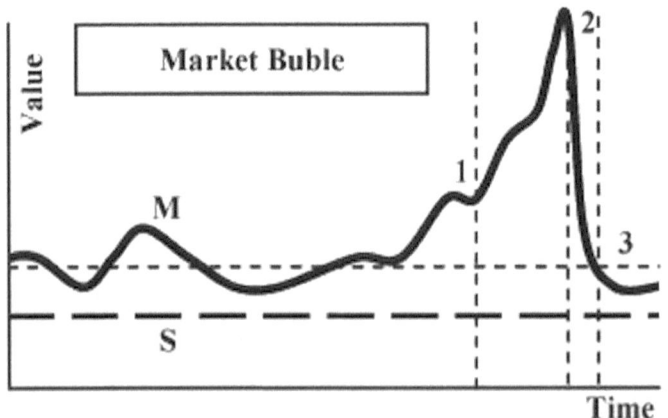

Where: M is current market price; S is substantial value; 1 is time when bubble starts to grow; 2 is the time when it starts to bust; 3 is where current market value is back to its medium value.

13 How to reduce Democracy Quality Inefficiency

Democracy Quality Inefficiency is a democratic phenomenon that occurs because of system and social agents actions. And involves classes of work, service or products that become inefficient or deficient to attend whatever is required from them. And imposed losses reach classes of agents because of that.

So the first big challenge someone who wants to counter quality inefficiency faces is to detect the classes of attributes among the infinite number of them, where it may be happening.

The second big challenge is to undo all the bad legislation that may be causing it, and create new legislation with qualified requirements that may stop it from continuing to happen.

These two challenges alone represent an important risk in the same way selective actions present. Because it is a future situation that nobody comprehends in its infinite coordinates that must be constructed forcibly from another situation that have infinite coordinates.

Indeed market and political interests may lead to other bubble situations that have to be dealt with later. And deficient or inefficient systems may simply go from one bubble to another bubble in a never ending cycle. That simply may continue forever imposing losses on people.

After that is successfully obtained, comes the very expensive process of democracy social inefficiency reduction, exactly as we have exposed before.

So, the problem with disqualification gain is that prior government and market quality may have to be restored some day. And when we need to construct a higher social quality through legislation and proper market means; it is far more expansive than whatever we may have received when we disqualified it. At the end of the day, it is far more expansive to construct anything then it is to destroy.

CHAPTER 16

DEMOCRATIC QUALITATIVITY

Interactive Class Effects – constitute "real class objects" of interactive waves that may be observed in day to day reality, most of the time as disconnected phenomenons. In the prior two chapters we considered interactive waves and correspondent interactive class effects of; Secondary Assistance; Differentiation Market and Democracy Inefficiency. In this chapter we shall discuss Democratic Quality and Qualitativity.

01 Democratic Quality

Democratic Quality - is the level of democratic characteristics that are present in the day to day dimension of a proper rule system.

The objective theory accepts the idea that perfect democratic systems are organized as an object.

That is necessary, because there is no king, or any other sovereign to command it, except people themselves, who are at the same time sovereign and consequent agents of these systems. And all these people need also to tackle their own individual interests in day to day dimension.

Because of this, all democratic proper rule systems, need to work alone as a machine, that are only commanded and eventually fixed by their owners from time to time.

The only way to get this done in a perfect mode is through the use of **Democratic Characteristics** within the system.

They work together, one complimenting the other; if one is defective; all the others go the same way. When all of them are present in the system in their full extent then we have a **perfect democratic system**.

For a variety of reasons explained in prior chapters and books, these **perfect democratic systems** work with the most efficiency and adaptability.

Consequently, they work with the least possible cost, and conceptually no imposed loss whatsoever. But there is no perfect democratic system in reality. Notwithstanding that it serves well as a parameter so that we may identify and evaluate any other system.

Any real proper rule system may be considered to be an imperfect democratic system.

However the level of democratic characteristics that are present in their day to day dimension may be very much different, one to the other.

Here we refer only to **democratic differences**, not to any other differences that also may be present.

Conceptually in all imperfect democratic systems there are imposed losses, which ones are greater as they get far away from the democratic principles. And these imposed losses trigger systemic differentiation processes that diminish, or inflate, their aspect's values. And that is registered in market current prices or other democracy results.

02 Measuring Democratic Quality

2.1 - Rules and Order

When we create a proper rule system we want it to transform "thoughts" into "real class objects".

But when a system materializes any object in reality, the "thoughts" that were supplied to it, end up being changed by its very interaction with social and natural "thoughts" that also interfere in reality materialization.

That means "resulting thoughts" that really produce things in a proper rule system, normally are different from the "thoughts" we officially, have supplied the system with.

We call **Legal Base**, or **Set of Rules** to the "thought expressions" officially supplied to a proper rule system. And we call **Democratic Order** or **Democratic Thinking** to the "abstract thoughts" that really command day to day reality formation.

2.2 - Rules and order differences

There are many differences between the set of rules and the democratic order; including the following:

Formation

A set of rules is formed by society – that is, will of participants or those who represent them - and is enforced into the system through official practices.

While a democratic order is created by the natural order of things, in a process that considers not only the proper rule system environment and its dynamics but also, all other existential environments with their particular structures and dynamics.

No one can stop this natural process of a democratic order formation, that is different from the legal base we have supplied to the proper rule system; but we may take that into consideration in our calculations to think and realize objectives in any proper rule system. That is exactly what the Objective theory does.

Aspects

A set of rules, no matter its size, it has only a limited number of aspects and commands.

While the democratic order, is composed of infinite aspects and commands that are necessary to govern all parts of "real things".

Rank

A set of rules do not necessarily relate to reality, it is simply a set of words written in some natural or even virtual means. We may say it is addressed to the "mental environment of those ones, who will enforce it".

While the democratic order, relates directly to reality and has the lowest rank among the other sets of existence orders. That means it may be changed not only by the rule system itself, but also by society or nature orders automatically.

Environment

The set of rules is a social phenomenon that is studied by Juridical Sciences.

While democratic order is a proper rule environment exclusive phenomenon; which does not exist in society, and is studied exclusively by Objective Theory Sciences – or **Objective-Democracy Sciences**.

2.3 - Analogy

We may say that any real proper rule system has a unique set of intrinsic characteristics that control all its relation with day to day dimension.

And they relate not only with system basic principles and values, but also to all other existential principles and values on the reality around it.

Than all we have to do is analyze these intrinsic characteristics to discover the presence of the democratic characteristics.

The following analogy will explain how we may do this:
Consider the set of cars shown in the following figure's 48 upper part:

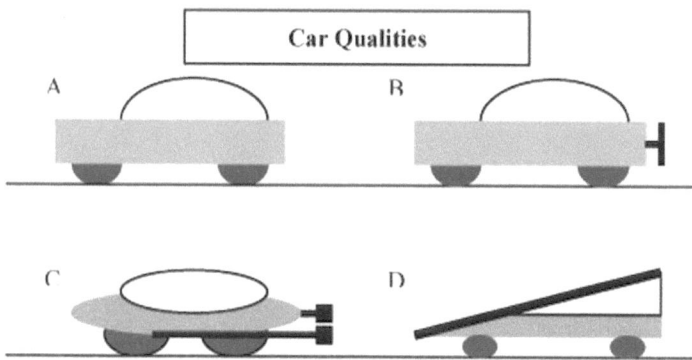

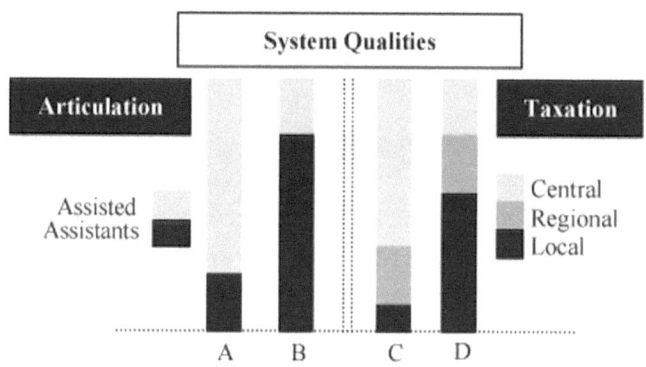

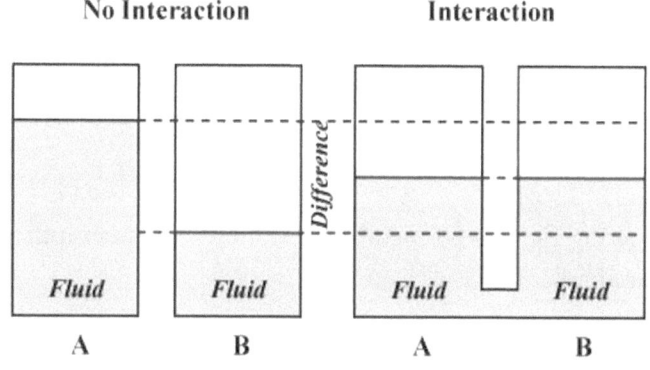

In this figure's 48 upper part we show you 4 different types of cars. Each one of them has a series of characteristics that are intrinsic to its model. Shape, structure and composition of each car determine these different characteristics. They are independent from human opinion.

03 Quality Classes

We may separate some of these characteristics as follows:

Substantial characteristics are the ones relative to values; such as size and weight.

Adjective characteristics are the ones relative to classes; such as thoughts, and ideas.

Imponderable characteristics are the ones relative to external actions over values and classes; such as intensions, care, and jealousy of the owner.

04 Quality Classes in a System

Real democratic systems are also organized as an object. So, they also have intrinsic characteristics that we may find.

To discover their democratic characteristic we simply relate some of their aspects one with the other, and compare each relation to a correspondent abstract one in a perfect democratic system.

Some of these relations constitute classes with specific names and are used as indicators. We may classify a system with respect to any relation or indicator.

The following figure's 48 meddle part, shows 4 system indicators that we can analyze.

Articulation is the relation between people that receives government subsidy to the total number of participants in a proper rule System.

- A- The articulation indicator shows us, that system A is controlled by Class (Assisted). They constitute their imponderable factor; and we may call it "support system".

- B- The articulation indicator tells us that System B is controlled by Class (Assistant); they are their imponderable factor; and we may call it a "solidarity system".

Relative Taxation is the relation between the existing taxation in a government system that exists inside other system, and the sum of all taxation contained in that other system.

System C is controlled in relative taxation indicator by class (Central Government); Central authorities are their imponderable factor. It is a **Differentiation System.** System D is controlled in relative taxation aspect by the class (Local Government); Local authorities are their imponderable factor. It is a **local service system-** we also may call it **a condominium democracy.**

As we can see, democratic principles are intensely present in the democratic aspects analyzed in systems B and D – Responsibility is well observed in system B; and Sovereign Power (democratic agent's authority) is well preserved in system D. Indeed this must come from one single more efficient system. In more efficient systems, all democratic indicators point to a very intense presence of democratic principles.

Quite in the contrary, in systems A and B the authority power is very much evident telling us that this may come from one whole system that is inefficient or even deficient.

That is the way we can identify democratic characteristics presence in as many relations or indicators as we may desire. But conversion principles move excess values through out the system, making all subsystems give the same answer as to democratic level. That means conceptually we will not find a more efficient subsystem operating alongside a deficient subsystem. That means if one subsystem is deficient all others tend to be deficient too.

05 Qualitativity

Given a certain democratic quality, when a proper rule system interacts with another, their differences in quality level will become an imponderable factor that will introduce objective values in each one of them. We call these values **qualitativity**.

Qualitativity is an **objective factor** introduced in a proper rule system when it interacts with a quality different system. For instance, when a psychologist individual proper rule system and patient individual proper rule system interact; qualitativity in the patient may be his cure, and in the psychologist may be her time, and whatever resources she may have spent in the process. To compensate it, she demands cash payment.

In another example, if a "miss behaving student", suddenly "cries very loudly" in the classroom, and disturbs all his classmates; **qualitativity** is that "screen"; and **quality difference** is his "miss behavior" with respect to all other students. It is an imponderable factor because no one knows what it may produce.

Qualitativity is so important that people in all societies have a saying like this one; "tell me who your fiends are, and I'll tell you who you are!" And that's exactly because there is a natural pressure for their social qualities to converge in spite of the fact they constitute different individual proper rule systems.

5.1 – Analogy Water Containers

We may compare what happens in systems with different quality levels that interact with each other, to what happens when two fluid containers with different fluid levels interact with each other. The following figure's 48 lowers part, explains this thought.

Notice that independently, systems "A" and "B", maintain their different fluid levels without any disturbance. But when the two systems interact; an imbalance appears in both systems; that pressures the highest fluid level toward the lowest and the lowest fluid level toward the highest. All are stable again when both systems have the same fluid level.

06 Democratic Qualitativity

That same natural behavior seen in this figure repeats itself, when two democratically different systems are interacting with each other. By other side:

Democratic Qualitativity is an **objective factor** that is introduced on a proper rule system when it interacts with a democratically different system. So, when two proper rule systems interact with each other, the democratic differences between them become an active imponderable factor that introduces **objective factors** in each of them. These objective factors are called **qualitativity.**

In **the "same fluid" case**, both levels end up equating each other in an **efficient equilibrium** due to their homogeneity and singularity. But in a real democratic system, **qualitativity** causes its environment to be initially imbalanced and consequently systemic differentiation to appear, in order to restore **just equilibrium** within the whole **existence environment**.

07 Class Analyses

Let us consider that something is being sold in a market for 10 monetary units. Then someone comes with the same product at the price of one monetary unit to sell in this same market. Consider that the only difference in his product is its source, which was an underdeveloped country with very low democratic quality. **Qualitativity** is exactly that difference. Indeed people are paying less because they are bringing into their system that negative **qualitativity**. That difference will instantaneously become a selective like, **differential objective factor** that will trigger **systemic differentiation** to start and continue in that market, until a lower **stable democratic quality – just equilibrium** – is reached. Lower democratic quality may mean higher unemployment, lower work pay, industry closure, etc…

But **democratic qualitativity** itself occurs in some specific circumstances. When one product or service is traded, it may present some differences with relation to the market. For instance it may be e new product; it may be socially more efficient, it may be socially preferred because of its color, design or whatever. Nothing of this constitutes **democratic qualitativity** – although they may constitute other types, which are not discussed in this book; for instance, social, or natural. So, **democratic qualitativity** implies there is no other difference at all, from a service or product that is being traded in the market, except its origin; of course, another rule system with a different democratic quality. It is constituted solely as a result of existing differences among democratic levels in the systems that are interacting.

08 Qualitativity Consequences

8.1 - Increase market results

According to the Objective Theory when we have two proper rule systems interacting, one is society of the other, together with all that may exist between the two. So we may also say that:

Qualitativity is a result of society interaction with a proper rule system. In such situation quality differences travel through society to get to our considered system. The figure's 49 upper part, explains this thought.

Where: M is market current price; M_1 is market offered price; M_2 is market differentiated price. As we can see positive qualitativity is only a fraction of negative qualitative, the other fraction is gain for the dealers, in the process.

We may conclude that when we allow negative qualitativity, to enter our system; than market agents gain profit for this. So, it is a good thing for market results. That is exactly why business people have no objections to it. They simply use it.

8.2 - Increase Social Differences

When we accept negative qualitativity into the system, we cause disqualification to appear in its social market standards, and consequently social differences to grow as a result. The following figure's 49 meddle part explains this effect.

8.3 - Increase Democratic Inefficiency

By the democratic side, qualitativity works exactly as selective differentiation that is imposed on to the market by its own players. And it is exactly because of this characteristic that it may be controlled by authorities; or simply accepted as it is. Once it is in the system; then it transforms itself into systemic differentiation which is out of government control. Nobody is completely able to define what the precise consequences of negative qualitativity will be; because of its infinite ramifications.

8.4 - Increase Social Inefficiency

When someone enters the market with negative qualitativity advantage, this person may be able to commercially defeat all others in that market. To those who are not selling negative qualitativity, simply two options are left; close their business, or change activity to survive. That means qualitativity sellers grow at the expense of others demise. And also means that disqualified systems are able by selling negative qualitativity, to push down more qualified systems; the greater their disqualification the greater may be their advantages. But the closing of business or even the change in market economic structure ends up letting people without, or stuck in low paying jobs. That is exactly an increase in social inefficiency.

09 Qualitativity Protection

More qualified systems need to protect themselves from negative qualitativity sellers. If they do not do this, social disqualification is inevitable; and the button for this process in an international context is very low. Indeed it is established by the more deficient systems in the world.

But qualitativity protection is not as easy as we could think of at the start. Let's do some simple considerations on this matter as we move on. Consider we have a central system and inside it several other regional systems. The figure's 49 lower part illustrates this thought.

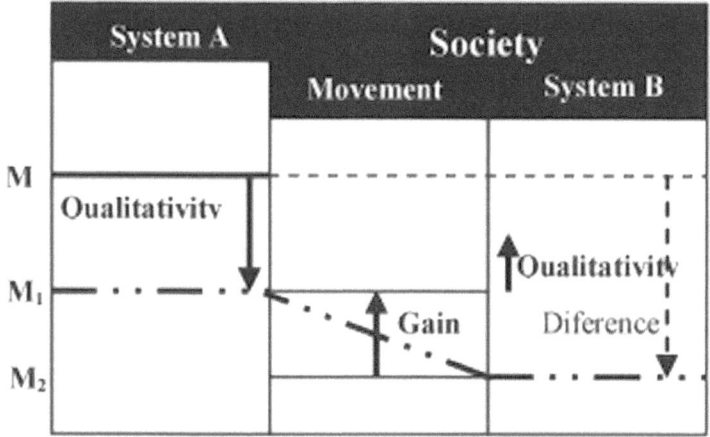
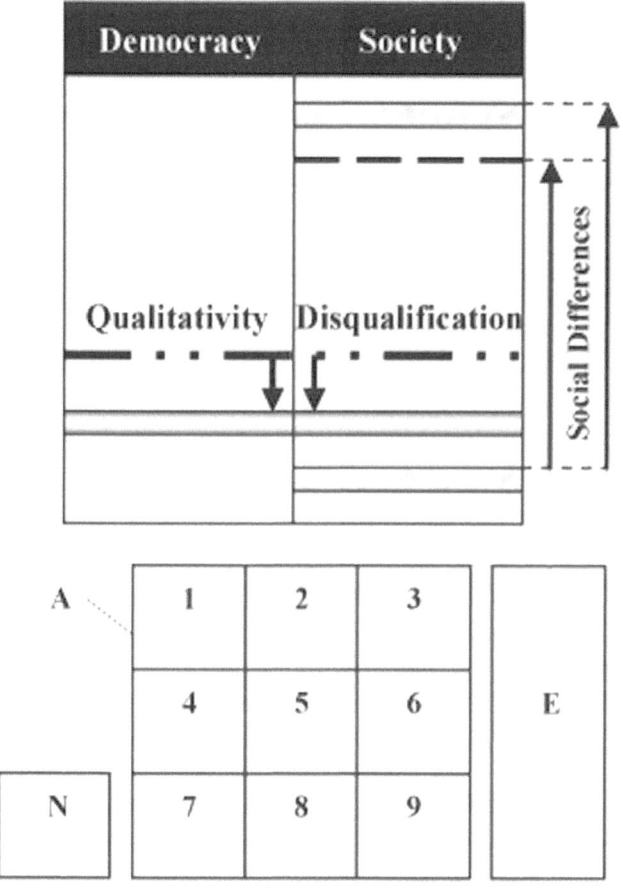

In this illustration we have system N that is disqualified and wants to introduce negative qualitativity into system A. System A is subdivided into 9 subsystems; 1 to 9. And also, we have system E that is neighbor of system A. The options in system A to counter qualitativity are as follows:

1. If only one of the regions counters qualitativity; it may enter in all other regions. And after disqualifying each one of them it transforms itself in systemic differentiation end finally takes on the defender.

    As an example, let us say that region 5 in system A, takes all the appropriate measures to counter negative qualitativity coming from system N. But system N continues its relation with all the other regions, and of course puts negative qualitativity in each one of them. Because of this, systemic differentiation starts in all these regions and also of course invades and installs itself in region 5 – this may occur in the infinite values that are or may be shared among region 5 and all others.

2. If by other way, central system A decides to force qualitativity sellers to use the same current prices in the market, then we have disqualification of market structure any way, which converts itself into social and systemic inefficiency. For example let us say your country decides to import everything from abroad, were could you find a job, and how many people would be seeking job in your country?

3. If central system A imposes a tax on products and services coming from system N, then it may neutralize direct qualitativity imposition, and may use tax proceeds, to counter disqualification effects.

4. But suppose system N sells its product to system E; which is not defending itself against qualitativity; and system E puts it into another product and then sells it to system A; in this case qualitativity is entering system A though system E.

These are some of the important problems we face when we want to defend ourselves against qualitativity. Notice that "qualitativity protection", do not confound itself with "market protection" because on this case a more competitive product is barred from the market, and in the "qualitativity protection" case; a disqualified product is barred from disqualifying a more qualified market.

CHAPTER 17

SYSTEM ANALYSES

01 Study of System and its Behavior

Objective Democraciology presents two main study areas for analyzing systems and their behavior, which ones are, Objective Systemiology and Objective Existential Dynamics as follows:

Objective Systemiology - studies structural characteristics of proper rule systems. It is divided into three study sub areas as follows:

Objective Democracy – studies all relative situations in a particular objective environment.

Objective Consequence is an "abstract class object" constituted by all situations in a particular environment collectively referred to.

Objective Politics – studies all imponderable factors that are changing a proper rule environment at a particular time.

Objective Regime is an "abstract class object" constituted by all the imponderable factors that affect a proper rule environment at a particular time collectively referred to. If only a group of aspects are being affected by all considered imponderable factors, we call them collectively by **Objective Police**. Both Objective Regime and Objective Polices may receive a label that identifies a particular type of condition.

Objective Administration studies the necessary changes in regime or situation to achieve other values, and the means to do the change. **Objective Change** is all the changes collectively necessary to get a proper rule system to a specific situation and condition.

<u>Objective Existential Dynamics</u> - studies dynamics characteristics and evolution of existential environment in time. It is divided into several other sub areas, including:

Personal Dynamics studies democratic agent's equilibrium in the existential environment.

Environmental Dynamics studies democratic environment's equilibrium in the existential or life environment.

System analyses should be conducted by a popular sovereign, rather then by any authority. Because at the end of the day; it is authority's work that is being evaluated.

The Lira Method of Democratic Evaluation is adequate to conduct Systemiology analyses. It consists in dividing each aspect value by another or performing any other calculation, and then comparing the result to a similar perfect system aspect relation or calculation. Some of these relations or calculations are labeled and considered as indicators. As time passes relation moves exposing to us the imponderable factors that are changing the system in the considered aspects. By the other side, we need Lirian Mathematics to conduct dynamic analyses. Let us use it to calculate equilibrium in some situations or environments.

02 Equilibrium

2.1 - Democratic Personal Equilibrium

At any given moment the Objective Consequence is changing so slowly, that it may be considered stabilized. That tells us the system is in an equilibrium state. Let us establish democratic equilibrium based upon the responsibility indicator. **Responsibility** is the obligation for a participant to pay expenses he causes.

There are two responsibility regime classes – through which responsibility is formed - accepted in Objective Democraciology. They are; Efficient Equilibrium Regime and Just Equilibrium Regime.

2.2 - Efficient Equilibrium Regime

In an efficient equilibrium regime every obligation is bound to an equivalent right. The indicator stays like this:

$$O = R$$

Where: O = Obligation; R = Right; the Efficient State Model uses a modified form of this regime to allow some time for the equation to balance in some cases; such as solidarity. Notice that Efficient State Model may do almost everything a Just State Model may do, only more efficiently.

2.3 - Just Equilibrium Regime[1]

In just equilibrium regime the relation **obligation** to **right** is established by a justice maker authority. The indicator stays like this:

$$O = R_{Just}$$

$$R_{Just} = R - R_1 \cdot Will_{Government}$$

Where: O = Obligation; R = Right; R_{Just} is a value that is different from A but is imposed by the will of a stronger agent; R_1 is an objective value introduced into the equation by the imponderable factor; $Will_{Government}$ is an imponderable factor that represents the will of an authority with

---
[1] You find more information about Responsibility Regimes in this book chapter Systemic Differentiation – section "Important causes for Systemic Differentiation"

exclusive state power who is able to impose his will and change the value of R in its relation to O (active=1; inactive=0).

03 System Reality Equilibrium

3.1 - Democratic Social Equilibrium

As we know the democratic environment is only a part of reality. Through democracy freedom, the system interacts with society. Through this interaction society introduces value in the equation to compensate the aggressiveness. The following equation explains this thought.

$$O = R - R_1 \cdot \text{Will}_{Government} + R_2 \cdot \text{Will}_{Market}$$

Where: R_2 is an objective factor introduced in the equation by the imponderable factor. Will_{Market} is an imponderable factor that represents the will of social agents to react against any imbalance imposed on the equilibrium equation against them (active=1; inactive=0).

Notice that in this equation; still equilibrium is reached with R_{Just} different from O. It may be higher or much lower.

3.2 - Democratic Social Equilibrium

In real systems yet another component appears in this equation that is "inefficiency". The class equation stays like this:

$$O = R - R_1 \cdot \text{Will}_{Government} + R_2 \cdot \text{Will}_{Market} - R_3 \cdot \text{Effect}_{Inefficiency}$$

Where: R_3 is an objective value introduced in the equation by inefficiency imponderable factor. $\text{Effect}_{Inefficiency}$ is an imponderable factor that represents the combined effect of all objective inefficiencies that are present in the system.

Government has the exclusive state power to impose differentiation values, and market has the market power to correct it. Since every factor in this equation is free from the other, government may never be able to force imposed losses on the market. And market agents are free to jump out of the market, if this becomes their desire.

This equation tells us that the appropriate use of selective differentiation by aggressive authorities must supersede market influence and inefficiency effect. This necessity induces deficient or inefficient governments to constantly increase their imbalances, repressions, and censoring against markets in search of a match that simply may never come.

3.3 - Democratic Existential Equilibrium

But reality is a part of a greater environment that includes unreality as well. Thoughts and Decisions also may introduce objective values in the personal equilibrium equation and change its equilibrium values. The democratic – existential equilibrium equation stays like this.

$$O = R - R_1 \cdot \text{Will}_{Government} + R_2 \cdot \text{Will}_{Market} - R_3 \cdot \text{Effect}_{Inefficiency} + R_4 \cdot \text{Will}_{Thoughts} + R_5 \cdot \text{Will}_{Decisions}$$

Where: R (3 and 4) are objective factors introduced by Will (Thoughts and Decisions); which are imponderable factors that represent ones will to change things (active=1; inactive=0).

This existential equilibrium equation tells us that in a Just State Model agents use their thoughts and decisions in order to maximize their gains or support lesser imposed losses. Exactly because of this characteristic, autocratic system environments tend to align all agents will and decisions to that one in control of the system.

3.4 - Democratic Life Imbalance

Notice that life experience for any considered person is an imbalanced wave. Someone may gain with life others may lose. In some aspects as the natural ones, it follows well defined patters of gains and losses;

in others, it is up for each agent to maximize or minimize his or her experience in life.

04 Environmental Equilibrium

But equilibrium also occurs when we consider each environment separately. The class equation for environmental existential equilibrium is defined as follows:

$$G_{Disposable} = G_{Government} + G_{Market}$$

Where: $G_{Disposable}$ is the same concept as PIB; $G_{Government}$ are tax collected by government; and G Market is market gain net of $G_{government}$. But $G_{Government}$ is this:

$$G_{Government} = G_{Services} + G_{Assistance}$$

Where: $G_{Service}$ are values returned to those ones who have paid them to the government; $G_{Assistance}$ are values delivered by government to those who did not pay. Also G_{Market} is this:

$$G_{Market} = G_{Capital} + G_{Work} + M_{Material}$$

Where: $G_{Capital}$ are interest and profit gained on the market; G_{Work} are salaries and other labor payments gained on the market; and $M_{Material}$ are material value expenditures made in excess. Substituting values in the environmental equilibrium equation we have that:

$$G_{Disposable} = G_{Services} + G_{Assistance} + G_{Capital} + G_{Work} + M_{Material}$$

Than we may establish environmental equilibrium equation as a function of work payments as follows:

$$G_{Work} = G_{Disposable} - G_{Capital} - G_{(Assistance + Services)} - M_{Material}$$

This equation tells us that government intervention, capital returns, and market material fluctuations - in price or quality - affects work payment. But service is part of personal equilibrium class equation:

$$R = G_{Services} + M_{Services}$$

Where: R is the right to consumption; $G_{Services}$ are services delivered by government. $M_{Services}$ are services delivered by the free market.

Notice that, if government services are cheaper than market services than we have an efficiency gain in the personal consumption equation. But otherwise if it is more expansive than that, we have an inefficiency imposed loss in that same equation.

By other side, these analyses for $G_{Services}$ do not stand for $G_{Assistance}$ which is simply an imposed loss on those who work.

05 Introduction to Objective Politics

5.1 - Proper Rule System Regimes

As we have seen this is the democratic equilibrium class equation:

$$O = R - R_1 \cdot \text{Effect}_{Inefficiency} - R_2 \cdot \text{Will}_{Government} - R_3 \cdot \text{Will}_{Market}$$

Considering that, electors participate in elections as democratic agents; but express their will in the ballot boxes as social agents (Notice that there is no law regulating electors' thoughts). We may say that authorities are connected and influenced by these elector's decisions. Therefore it is possible to classify the various regimes according to the articulation indicator which measures relation between agents and authorities, as follows:

  6 - Perfect Democracy Regime
  5 - Plain Democracy Regime
  4 - Sovereign Sociocracy Regime

3 - Dependent Sociocracy Regime
2 - Dominant Autocracy Regime
1 - Dictatorship Regime

Let us describe them shortly:

Perfect Democracy Regime – occurs when all imponderable factors are inactive. This regime class, never materializes because inefficiencies are always present in real systems, due to a variety of existence factors. But it serves well as a fixed reference for all real democratic systems.

Plain Democracy Regime – occurs when, less than 20% of participants are dependent on government support.

In this regime class participant's rights depend on inefficiency and market factors, but solidarity may be used to improve system utility. **Solidarity** is when a majority of participants voluntarily decides to pay some of a minority's government bills to increase system utility. Social influences are kept as opposition rhetoric.

Sovereign Sociocracy Regime - occurs when, between 20% and less than 50% of participants are dependents on government support.

Social and democratic influences are present in this regime class but democratic influence is greater; and so, its followers may introduce democratic conservative orders to improve systems quality in order to accommodate some of the progressivism follower's demands.

Specific preponderant democratic influences – such as labor valuation, sovereign valuation, responsibility valuation - may give additional labels to these systems.

Dependent Sociocracy Regime – occurs when, between 50% and less than 80% of participants are dependents on government support.

Social Influence is present and preponderant in this regime class; because of this, system's objective may shift to attend any preponderant social interest; which one is, not certain, not completely defined, nor well-founded, and may change without any record. And so, progressivism followers may introduce imbalanced orders to accommodate social influences. These preponderant social influences may give additional social labels to systems under this regime. Some of these influences have known social labels, and even known creators; however many others are not socially identified yet; and are not socially labeled.

Dominant Autocracy Regime – occurs when 80% or more of participants are dependants on government support.

Social influence is present but government may choose what to enforce against what classes of participants. Literally everything depends on interpretation of authorities; such as liberties, responsibilities, rule of laws, sovereignty, and submission. Everything is on the table for authority interpretation, decision and enforcement. Under this regime class Election Day may bring a dispute between electors and authorities concerning some specific decisions already made by authorities. The real characteristics that are being materialized by the system under this regime class may give them additional social or even natural label.

Dictatorship Regime- occurs when there is no participant free of government support.

In such regime class, authorities may substitute all social influence for their own will. And they may enforce their will against all participants using autocratic mode systems.

The following figure illustrates the 6 main regime classes discussed in this text.

SYSTEM ANALYSES

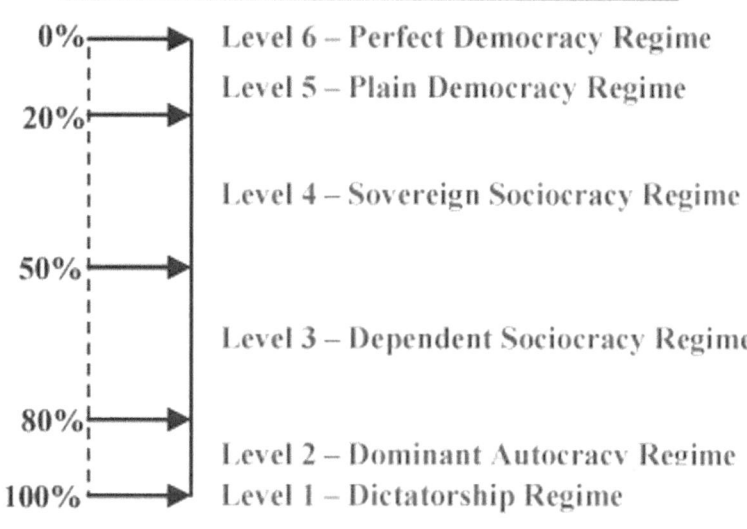

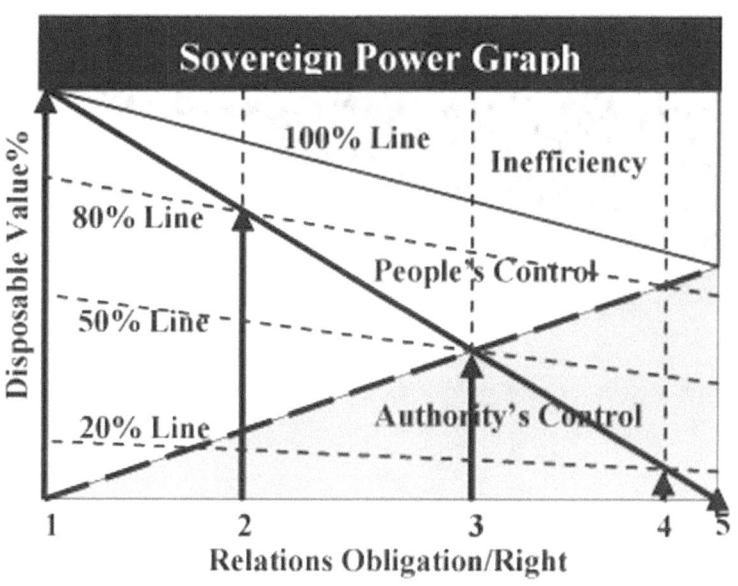

Situation 1, is a Perfect Democracy Regime; situation 1 until 2 are Plain Democracy Regimes; situation 2 until 3 are Sovereign Sociocracy Regimes; situation 3 until 4 are Dependent Sociocracy Regimes; situation 4 until 5 are Dominant Autocracy Regimes; and situation 5 is a Dictatorship Regime.

According to the natural order of things, as authorities assume sovereign power inefficiency grows and destroys part of disposable value. In a perfect democracy regime, inefficiency is nonexistent; and in a dictatorship regime it is in maximum value; the exact objective number in all these specific classes depend on each real case.

BIBLIOGRAPHY

Objective Democracy Study Area Books:
They are Democraciology and Lira Method of Objective Evaluation books.

LIRA, J. Edson de Souza. Democracia Participativa Condominial: Teoria objetiva do sistema democrático de governo. Recife - Brazil: PL Edições, 2006. (First book of Objective Democraciology)

_____. Jogo Democrático Objetivo no seu dia-a-dia. São Paulo- Brazil: Sortecci, 2006.

_____. Jogo dos Atuantes: Assistencialismo Favelização e Guerra Urbana. Recife. Edição independente do autor. 2007. 78 páginas.

_____, Estado Eficiente ou Estado Justo? A escolha é sua. São Paulo- Brazil: Sortecci, 2008.

Books that were consulted amongst many others;

Pearce, John A; Formulation and Control of Competitive Strategy/ John A Pearce II, Richard B Robinson, Jr: 6th Edition Irwin/ McGraw-Hill; 1997

Adobe Dreamweaver' CSS Classroom in a book; translation Igor Vianna; technical revision : Marcio Vitale- Porto Alegre; Bookmam, 2012.

Economics for Dummies; by Sean Masaki Flinn; published by Willey Publishing inc: Hoboken – NJ USA ; 2005.

Many others in areas like:

Civil Engineering – complete superior graduation.
Computer Programing
Economics
Mathmatics (linear Algebra, Calculus, Derivatives, Quantum Phisics etc...)
Law (Brazilian, and USA Central Union)
Sociology
Religion
Human History
Political Science

Notice that God doeth not create new principles when men discover new areas of study; All natural principles are there, just acting inside all areas of study. Many of these principles where brought into the Objective Theory from other areas of study. Also notice that in short we may say that:

Objective Theory is a combination of simple mathematics, logic and good sense.